PAKISTAN

ABDO
Publishing Company

PAKISTAN

by Pete Heiden

Content Consultant
Professor Saeed Shafqat, Director, Centre for Public Policy and Government,
Forman Christian College, Lahore, Pakistan

CREDITS

Published by ABDO Publishing Company, 8000 West 78th Street, Edina, Minnesota 55439. Copyright © 2012 by Abdo Consulting Group, Inc. International copyrights reserved in all countries. No part of this book may be reproduced in any form without written permission from the publisher. The Essential Library™ is a trademark and logo of ABDO Publishing Company.

Printed in the United States of America,
North Mankato, Minnesota
062011
092011

 THIS BOOK CONTAINS AT LEAST 10% RECYCLED MATERIALS.

Editor: Melissa York
Copy Editor: Susan M. Freese
Series design and cover production: Emily Love
Interior production: Kazuko Collins

About the Author: Pete Heiden is a freelance writer in Minneapolis, Minnesota.

Library of Congress Cataloging-in-Publication Data
Heiden, Pete.
  Pakistan / by Pete Heiden.
      p. cm. -- (Countries of the world)
  Includes bibliographical references and index.
  ISBN 978-1-61783-117-1
  1. Pakistan--Juvenile literature. 1. Title.
  DS376.9.H44 2011
  954.91--dc23
                                    2011020921

Cover: K2 summit, Karakoram mountain range, Pakistan

TABLE OF CONTENTS

CHAPTER 1
A VISIT TO PAKISTAN

Carefully wiping the lens on your spotting scope, you lean back, trying to breathe deeply and slowly. There are snow leopards in the mountains around you, and you would like to see one. The odds are against you— even here, at what's often called "the roof of the world." Magpies often scavenge leopard kills, and seeing a couple of them searching the rocks above had made you hopeful. But what you had thought was a resting leopard through the scope turned out to be a bushy plant. You have come to believe that in this high, rocky landscape, plants are almost as rare as leopards. Now, an hour of peering through the scope has made your head ache.

You have come to Khunjerab National Park, located on the border of Pakistan and China. This area between the Khunjerab River and Chapchingal Pass is rough and rocky, and the mountains you can see are unnamed peaks comprised of rock and snow. The famous peaks are all south of you, across miles of more mountains and glaciers. Overwhelmed

Camels are still used for transportation in the mountains of Pakistan.

ADVENTURE AWAITS

From Islamabad, travelers can reach the northern part of the country in two ways. The first and safest way is to take a one-hour flight from Islamabad to Gilgit. The second and more adventurous way involves a daylong road trip to the town of Gilgit, following the Grand Trunk Road northwest from Islamabad and Rawalpindi to Hasan Abdal, where it connects with the Karakoram Highway (KKH). From Hasan Abdal, the KKH runs northeast to Gilgit, the Khunjerab Pass, and China.

Much of the central core of the country—from Islamabad to Karachi and Peshawar to Lahore—is accessible by train. In fact, it's still possible to follow the old Silk Road through the Khyber Pass and to travel across the Thar Desert by steam engine on the original British-built railway system from the nineteenth and early twentieth centuries.

by the mountains, you sympathize with the golden marmots, which scamper into the rocky crevices seeking shelter as a golden eagle floats overhead. Yesterday, you were fortunate enough to see a small group of Himalayan ibex, including one with large and beautifully curved scimitar-shaped horns. Movement on the slope to the south catches your eye, and you swing the scope toward it.

No luck! It's just another marmot.

One of the highest-altitude parks in the world, Pakistan's Khunjerab National Park is located in the province of Gilgit

The roads through Pakistan's mountains barely allow for the passage of trucks.

Baltistan. Many snow leopards reside within the park's borders, along with other endangered species such as the Himalayan ibex, the Marco Polo sheep, and the brown bear. Siberian ibex and blue sheep are also found here. Some of the most biodiverse alpine habitats in Pakistan are found within this park, which is adjacent to China's Taxkorgan Natural Reserve.

In Gilgit Baltistan, three major mountain ranges meet: the Karakoram, the Hindu Kush, and the Himalayas. Many of the world's tallest mountains are found within this area, including Chogori. *Chogori*, or the "King of Mountains" in the Balti language, is the local name for K2, the second-highest mountain in the world.

Although the mountains are high and cold, the lush valleys of Gilgit Baltistan hold fertile orchards where apricot, cherry, apple, and mulberry trees fill the air with the scent of flowers in spring. In the valleys, people also grow almonds, walnuts, and pine nuts—all nourished with mineral-rich waters from the melting glaciers. According to the local people, eating the fresh fruits and drinking the clear waters allows residents of the Hunza River valley of northern Pakistan to reach extreme old age. The completion of the Karakoram Highway has opened up northern Pakistan, and it's now possible to drive from Islamabad to China by way of Khunjerab Pass. Completion of the road has also resulted in fast-food restaurants being available in remote areas, including the Hunza valley.

Saying good-bye to Khunjerab National Park, you take a side trip to Skardu along the Gilgit-Skardu road, which is said to be "the road that eats Jeeps."[1] The bumpy drive along the Indus River takes all day—and you're lucky the road is open at all. From Skardu, you stop in Deosai

National Park, created to protect some of Pakistan's last endangered brown bears. This is where adventure-seekers begin their strenuous trek up the Baltoro Glacier to the Concordia and K2 base camps, where climbers prepare to ascend some of the world's highest mountains. To return to Islamabad, you take the short flight from Skardu. The Skardu–Islamabad flight is better than a roller coaster, giving passengers thrills as the plane swoops through the narrow gorge of the Indus River.

You know that a visit to any part of the country offers something to see: festivals, markets, and arts and crafts. Most towns have a market or bazaar for shopping and purchasing local foods and crafts, and large cities, such as Lahore, Islamabad, and Karachi, also offer a great variety of food, music, and art.

SHANGRI-LA

The inaccessible valleys of the Karakoram Range led to rumors among Europeans of valleys where people lived peaceful lives and did not grow old. The idea of Shangri-La, an earthly paradise free from the pressures of modern life, comes from James Hilton's 1933 novel *Lost Horizon*. The concept of Shangri-La is akin to the Buddhist tradition of Shambhala, a mythical hidden paradise. The Shangri-La of Hilton's book was supposedly based in part on the Hunza River valley, located just north of Gilgit.

THE SOUTH

In the south, you have come to tour Karachi, Pakistan's largest city, largest airport, and largest seaport. This former capital of Pakistan is located in southern Sindh Province, a short distance northwest of the Indus River delta on the Arabian Sea. Karachi's numerous beaches—including Sandspit Beach, Clifton Beach, and Hawke's Bay Beach—offer not only picnicking and swimming but also horseback riding and even camel riding along the water's edge.

You visit Karachi's most important cultural attraction, the Mazar-e-Quaid, or National Mausoleum, which is the tomb of Pakistan's founder and first leader, Mohammed Ali Jinnah. The mausoleum sits atop an elevated platform, high above a geometric pattern of steps, walkways, pools, fountains, and gardens. Constructed from white marble and decorated with curved Moorish arches and copper grilles, the large square-based structure is topped with a dome, creating a large open and airy room. In the center of this room sits Jinnah's tomb, surrounded by an ornate fence and armed guards. Hanging above the tomb is a huge four-tiered chandelier, a gift from China. At night, spotlights in the surrounding park illuminate the white structure, making it strikingly visible for miles.

Karachi was the capital of Pakistan until 1959.

Mazar-e-Quaid, the tomb of Pakistan's founder, Mohammed Ali Jinnah

Political Boundaries of Pakistan

WELCOME TO PAKISTAN

Situated at a geographic crossroads of inhospitable deserts, the steppes and high mountains of Asia, and the fertile lowlands of the Indian subcontinent, Pakistan is steeped in history and legend. It has been a nexus of multiple civilizations dating back 9,000 years or more. The land has been host to numerous invaders, including Alexander III of Macedonia, known as "the Great," and Genghis Khan, leader of the Mongols. For centuries, the main trade routes between Europe and Asia followed the Silk Road through Pakistan's mountain passes, bringing ideas, skills, and religions, in addition to a vast trade in silks and spices.

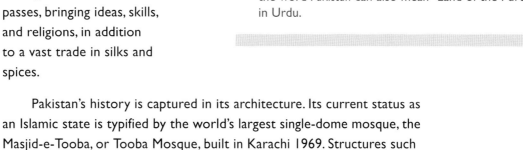

NAMING PAKISTAN

The area that is now Pakistan has been part of many empires throughout history. Calling the area Pakistan, however, is quite new. In 1933, a Muslim student at the University of Cambridge in England put together the first letters of the names of four provinces to form the new word: **P**unjab, **A**fghania (today called Khyber Pakhtunkhwa), **K**ashmir, and **I**ndus-Sindh (today called Sindh), plus the suffix – *stan* from the end of *Balochistan*. Serendipitously, the word *Pakistan* can also mean "Land of the Pure" in Urdu.

Pakistan's history is captured in its architecture. Its current status as an Islamic state is typified by the world's largest single-dome mosque, the Masjid-e-Tooba, or Tooba Mosque, built in Karachi 1969. Structures such as Saint Patrick's Cathedral and the Empress Market, both in Karachi,

DANGEROUS TRAVEL

Through the centuries, travelers along the Silk Road knew the risks of rivers, rockfalls, and deserts, as well as the dangers from local tribes, petty princes, and desperate bandits. Pakistan's roads may be in better condition today, but they are still often closed due to rockfalls, mudslides, and floods. In addition, the chance of being robbed, kidnapped, or killed remains a concern for travelers, as bandits and terrorists continue operating throughout much of Pakistan. As of 2011, the US State Department advised US citizens to avoid unnecessary travel to Pakistan.

date back to the British colonial period of the 1880s. Centuries of rule by India's Mughal Empire left ornate mosques, such as the Badshahi Mosque in Lahore. Pakistan's thousands of years of history are evident at ancient sites around the country such as Mehrgarh in Balochistan, Harappa and Taxila in Punjab, and Mohenjo Daro in Sindh.

A land with a glorious past, Pakistan is also a young country that has struggled politically and economically since its independence in 1947. High in population but lacking resources, Pakistan has difficulty feeding its people and negotiating peace among its many tribes and factions. Terrorist groups cause violence around the country, threatening citizens and foreigners alike. The people of Pakistan must find new ways to come together in order to end the violence, improve the standard of living, and face the challenges of today and tomorrow.

The Double-Headed Eagle stupa at Taxila, an important center of Buddhist study from the fifth century BCE to the second century CE

The people of Pakistan are striving for a more stable future.

SNAPSHOT

Official name: Islamic Republic of Pakistan (in Urdu, Islami Jumhuria Pakistan)

Capital city: Islamabad

Form of government: federal republic

Title of leader: prime minister (head of government); president (head of state)

Currency: Pakistani rupee (PKR)

Population (July 2011 est.): 187,342,721
World rank: 6

Size: 307,374 square miles (796,095 sq km)
World rank: 36

Language: Punjabi (most common), Urdu (official), English (official)

Official religion: Islam

Per capita GDP (2010, US dollars): $2,400
World rank: 179

CHAPTER 2

GEOGRAPHY: A RUGGED LAND

Pakistan is a rugged and rocky country with deserts, wetlands, and forested mountains. It is mostly arid. It is bordered by India to the east, China to the northeast, Iran to the southwest, and Afghanistan to the west and northwest. The Arabian Sea lies off its southern coast.

Pakistan has an area of 307,374 square miles (796,095 sq km), a little less than twice the size of California.[1] The terrain ranges from sandy beaches and mangrove forests along the Arabian Sea to sandy deserts, dry rocky plateaus, and fertile plains further inland to jagged uplands that climb swiftly into the high mountains. The summit of K2, located on Pakistan's northern border with China, reaches 28,251 feet (8,611 m).[2] The nation shakes with frequent

> The Karakoram Highway linking Pakistan and China opened in 1979.

The Indus River flows from the mountains down the length of Pakistan.

EARTHQUAKES

Pakistan, located where several landmasses collide, is seismically active, and earthquakes are a fact of life. Mud volcanoes and tsunamis are also caused by this seismic activity. In the earthquake that hit Pakistan in 1945, the collapse of an offshore mud volcano shortly after the quake may have caused the tsunami that was responsible for most of the deaths.

Five major earthquakes have hit Pakistan in recent times:

- May 30, 1935: A 7.5-magnitude quake destroyed Quetta in Balochistan and killed 30,000 people.

- November 27, 1945: In the Makran region in Balochistan, an 8.0-magnitude quake left 4,000 dead. Many are believed to have been killed by the resulting tsunami, which reached higher than 40 feet (12 m) in some locations.

- December 28, 1974: In northern Pakistan, a 6.2-magnitude quake killed 5,300 people.

- October 8, 2005: A 7.6-magnitude quake centered on Muzaffarabad in Azad Kashmir, just north of Islamabad, had a death toll of 86,000.

- October 28, 2008: In Balochistan, a 6.4-magnitude quake killed 166.[3]

and sometimes intense earthquakes.

A continental collision created the high mountains of northern Pakistan. Another tectonic collision is occurring in the southwest, just off the coast of Pakistan. In a process called subduction, the Arabian Plate is sliding under the Eurasian Plate. A frequent result of the subduction process is the creation of volcanoes. In the arid southwest of Pakistan, however, volcanoes do not produce lava and ash. Rather, they are mud volcanoes that occasionally spew spontaneously ignited fountains of methane gases high into the air.

REGIONS

Pakistan's landscape can be divided into a number of areas. The northern and western highlands contain the high mountains and valleys of the Himalayas, the Karakoram Range, and the Hindu Kush. Gilgit Baltistan, in northern Pakistan, is often called "the roof of the world" because of the height of its mountains. Pakistan's mountains, created by the collision of India into the continent of Asia, contain 40 of the world's 50 tallest peaks.[4]

Below the high northern mountains are long valleys blanketed in glaciers, and still lower lie narrow fertile valleys where people grow fruit and nut trees. The Indus River flows

MOUNTAIN FACTS

Of the 15 highest mountains in the world, six of them are located in Pakistan. Nanga Parbat is located in the Himalayas, and the other five are in the Karakoram Range.

Mountain	Height	World Rank
K2	28,251 feet (8,610 m)	2
Nanga Parbat	26,657 feet (8,125 m)	8
Gasherbrum I (K5)	26,470 feet (8,068 m)	11
Broad Peak (K3)	26,460 feet (8,065 m)	12
Gasherbrum II (K4)	26,401 feet (8,047 m)	14
Gasherbrum III	26,089 feet (7,952 m)	15[5]

Karachi lies on the coast of the Arabian Sea.

northwest through this area before turning south near Attock to neatly bisect Pakistan on its way to the sea. Important cities include Gilgit, Skardu, and Chitral in the far north and Peshawar in the northwest.

Several famous passes cut through the mountains, such as the Khunjerab Pass in the Northern Areas, the Khyber Pass in Khyber Pakhtunkhwa, and the Bolan Pass in Balochistan. These passes were important landmarks along the Silk Road and are steeped in the history of numerous invasions and migrations. Traders and troublemakers still use these important routes today.

PUNJAB

The word *Punjab* means "five waters" in the Persian language. The name refers to the five main rivers of Pakistan, which include the Indus River and its major tributaries—the Jhelum, Chenab, Ravi, and Sutlej Rivers—all of which flow through Punjab Province. The rivers converge with the Indus south of Multan before flowing into Sindh Province.

The Punjab and Sindh Plains border the Indus River and form the agricultural center of Pakistan. Using water from Punjab's rivers for irrigation, Pakistanis grow crops such as wheat, cotton, sugarcane, and rice. Lahore and Faisalabad in the north and Karachi in the south are the major cities. To the west of the Indus valley lies the Balochistan Plateau. Covering much of western and southwestern Pakistan, this area borders Iran and Afghanistan on the west and runs to the Arabian Sea in the

Geography of Pakistan

south. Traditionally the home of nomadic herders, the plateau is a dry, rocky, sandy high desert with little water, agriculture, or industry. Quetta is the major city of Balochistan.

To the east, bordering India, are the Thar and Cholistan Deserts, which are low, dry, and sandy. These deserts are some of the hottest and driest places on the earth. North of the plains, in Punjab, lies the Potwar Plateau, which has the highest annual rainfall of any area in Pakistan. This area lies adjacent to the high mountains between the Indus and Jhelum Rivers and runs south to the Salt Range, the location of the world's second-largest salt mine. The twin cities of Islamabad and Rawalpindi are located on the Potwar Plateau.

> The 2010 floods were the worst in the recorded history of Pakistan.

CLIMATE

The climate of Pakistan varies widely, from dry, hot deserts to temperate conditions in the northwest and to cold, arctic conditions in the high mountains of the north. The weather is dominated by the seasonal Asiatic monsoon. October and November is a transition period between the wet and dry seasons. The period from December through February is generally cool and dry, although temperatures in the mountains are quite cold. The following period, from March through May, is hot and dry. The summer months, July through September, bring the monsoon season, when the summer rains come. Very little rain falls in the southern desert.

Even though the Asiatic monsoon is the major climatic influence, that influence is not evenly felt across the country. For instance, Karachi, on the southern coast, generally gets less rain than Islamabad, which is farther north, even though Karachi is much more humid. The desert areas of the west, south, and southeast receive little rain year-round, remaining sunny and hot even during the monsoon. In the area around Karachi,

AVERAGE TEMPERATURES AND RAINFALL

Region (City)	Average January Temperature Minimum/Maximum	Average July Temperature Minimum/Maximum	Average Rainfall January/July
Plains (Islamabad)	36/61°F (2/16°C)	77/97°F (25/36°C)	2.5/9.2 inches (6.4/23.3 cm)
Desert (Jacobabad)	45/73°F (7/23°C)	86/109°F (30/43°C)	0.2/0.91 inches (0.5/2.3 cm)
Coast (Karachi)	55/77°F (13/25°C)	81/91°F (27/33°C)	0.04/0.3 inches (0.1/0.8 cm)
North (Peshawar)	39/63°F (4/17°C)	79/102°F (26/39°C)	1.4/1.3 inches (3.6/3.3 cm)[6]

A woman carries water in the Thar Desert.

MONSOONS

In casual speech, monsoon generally refers to the rainy season. Though the term *monsoon* is often used to describe rain, the word itself doesn't have anything to do with precipitation. A monsoon is a seasonal reversal in the direction of winds, and it can be said that the reversal of winds causes the dry season too. In winter, winds blowing over the deserts bring dry weather to much of the Indian subcontinent. But during the summer, those winds reverse direction, pushing moisture-filled air from the Arabian Sea inland over much of Pakistan and western India, causing the rainy season.

the average annual rainfall can be as little as 1 inch (2.5 cm), whereas farther north, Islamabad receives more than 40 inches (100 cm).[7] At times, however, the monsoon rains come with an intensity that creates devastating floods. The heavy rains that came in July and August 2010 caused major flooding, inundating 20 percent of Pakistan and killing approximately 1,600 people.[8]

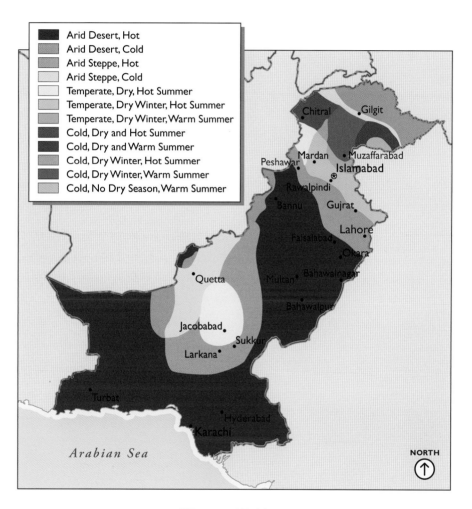

Legend:
- Arid Desert, Hot
- Arid Desert, Cold
- Arid Steppe, Hot
- Arid Steppe, Cold
- Temperate, Dry, Hot Summer
- Temperate, Dry Winter, Hot Summer
- Temperate, Dry Winter, Warm Summer
- Cold, Dry and Hot Summer
- Cold, Dry and Warm Summer
- Cold, Dry Winter, Hot Summer
- Cold, Dry Winter, Warm Summer
- Cold, No Dry Season, Warm Summer

Chitral • Gilgit
Mardan • Muzaffarabad
Peshawar • Islamabad ⊕
Rawalpindi
Bannu • Gujrat
Faisalabad • Lahore
• Okara
Quetta • Multan • Bahawalnagar
• Bahawalpur
Jacobabad •
Sukkur
Larkana •
• Turbat
• Hyderabad
Karachi

Arabian Sea

NORTH
↑

Climate of Pakistan

CHAPTER 3

ANIMALS AND NATURE: DIVERSE AND ELUSIVE

Pakistan has a wide variety of wildlife, yet few Pakistanis ever see it. Residents of large cities such as Karachi and Lahore are likely to see only domestic animals, such as donkeys and goats. Pakistanis' lack of contact with wildlife is due mostly to the fact that their country is quickly becoming urbanized, which means most species are few in number and limited in available habitat. Still, Pakistan holds a surprisingly large number of species, including as many as 174 species of mammals.[1]

The widest variety is found in the remote northern forests and mountains, including species of antelope, deer, bears, hyenas, and wild sheep and

Brown bears and Asiatic black bears are both found in Pakistan's mountains.

The markhor is an endangered animal.

Environmental organizations estimate there are only
4,000 to 6,500 snow leopards left in the world.

goats. Pakistan's national animal, the markhor goat, is found in the mountains near the Indus River. The snow leopard is an elusive mountain resident as well, as is the rhesus monkey. Multiple species of antelope and deer, as well as wild dogs and cats, live in the country's desert regions. In addition, a species of dolphin lives in the Indus River.

A number of reptiles are found in Pakistan, including two species of crocodiles: the marsh crocodile and the endangered gharial, both of which swim the waters of the Indus River. Pakistan has 72 species of snakes, of which 26 (12 terrestrial species and 14 marine species) are poisonous.[2]

SNOW LEOPARDS

Perhaps the most famous of Pakistan's wildlife is the snow leopard. Found across the mountains of central Asia, this endangered animal lives in Pakistan's harsh, cold, dry, and sparsely vegetated areas at high elevations. Preferring the steep, broken terrain of rock outcrops, cliffs, and ravines, these cats bed down where they can have a good view of the surrounding area. The cats' thick, smoky-gray fur with darker rosettes creates a pattern that makes them almost invisible in the rocks.

Male snow leopards weigh from 60 to 120 pounds (27 to 54 kg) and are much larger than the females. A big leopard may have a body longer than four feet (1.2 m), with a tail almost as long. These leopards like to hunt ibex and blue sheep, but they will eat whatever marmot or chukar they can catch.

Threats to snow leopards include poaching for their fur and their bones, which are used in traditional Asian medicine. In some areas, the loss of the cat's prey species from hunting and competition with livestock has been considerable. Herders also kill snow leopards that prey on their flocks.

NATIONAL ANIMALS OF PAKISTAN

Mammal: The markhor (*Capra falconeri*) is a wild goat with long, spiraling horns that are twisted tight like corkscrews. The males can have long, shaggy beards and manes and are much larger than the females.

Marine mammal: The Indus River dolphin (*Platanista minor*) has a long snout, rounded belly, stocky body, and large flippers. Generally between six and seven feet (1.8 and 2.1 m) in length, this dolphin tends to swim on its side and navigates with echolocation, as it is mostly blind.

Reptile: The marsh crocodile (*Crocodylus palustris*), also called the mugger crocodile, grows to 15 feet (4.6 m) in length and has the broadest snout of any crocodile species.

Amphibian: The Indus valley toad (*Bufo stomaticus*) is a light or dark mottled toad with an off-white belly.

Bird: The chukar partridge (*Alectoris chukar*), at 12 to 14 inches (30 to 36 cm) long, is a grouse-like bird that is mostly gray with black-striped sides. It has white cheeks and throat surrounded by a black band that crosses its red eyes like a mask.

Green and olive ridley sea turtles both can be found making nests on the Arabian Sea coast.

Eagles and vultures soar the skies throughout the country. Species of aquatic birds, including ducks, geese, and spoonbills, come to Manchhar Lake in Sindh. The Indus River is an important habitat for a wide variety of migrating birds.

FORESTS

Although only approximately 4 percent of Pakistan is forested, the country is home to diverse plant species.[3] An ancient juniper forest in Balochistan is thought to be one of the largest and oldest in the world. In Khyber

The thorny acacia tree grows in Pakistan's dry regions.

Pakhtunkhwa, a mixed collection of deodar cedar, pine, spruce, acacia, and oak can be found. Many species of fruit trees grow throughout the country.

Gilgit Baltistan is home to willow, pine, and fir trees, although large portions of the region lie barren above the tree line. Trees grow wherever they can find a foothold between the rocks and glaciers or human fields and orchards. Each spring brings a burst of color with the blooming of wildflowers.

Much of Sindh and Punjab are too dry for forests, other than scattered thorn forests of acacias, karir (a leafless shrub), and kandi (a flowering tree). In the south, mangrove forests are still found in the Indus River delta, along the coast.

ENVIRONMENTAL THREATS

Most of Pakistan's environmental issues are connected in obvious and not-so-obvious ways. For instance, agriculture destroys habitats by converting them into croplands, and overgrazing of livestock degrades the landscape and causes erosion. And while irrigation projects supply water to agricultural lands, they also take away habitat from endangered species such as the dolphin and the gharial. The few remaining dolphins struggle with agricultural pesticides, among other pollutants.

In arid locations such as Balochistan, age-old water systems are being replaced by modern water pumping. The modern technology is mining reserves of groundwater far in excess of their ability to recharge. This extensive removal of groundwater is causing the water tables to fall. However, in much of the Indus River valley agricultural area, the opposite is occurring. Overwatering and leakage from irrigation canals is causing the widespread waterlogging of soil and an accumulation of salts, making the land unfit for plant growth.

The widespread use of the drug diclofenac, used to treat livestock, has caused a decline in a number of birds, especially vultures. A bird scavenging on the carcass of a cow that was treated with diclofenac will soon die from acute renal failure, as its kidneys will quit functioning. This use of diclofenac has decimated populations of scavengers, quickly reducing once-common birds such as the Oriental white-backed and long-billed vultures to the point they are now endangered. Civil unrest and fighting in Pakistan's

ENDANGERED SPECIES IN PAKISTAN

According to the International Union for Conservation of Nature (IUCN), Pakistan is home to the following numbers of species that are categorized by the organization as Critically Endangered, Endangered, or Vulnerable:

Mammals	23
Birds	26
Reptiles	10
Amphibians	0
Fishes	33
Mollusks	0
Other Invertebrates	15
Plants	2
Total	109[4]

northwest has seriously threatened one of Pakistan's wild goats, the Chiltan markhor.

Pakistan's forests are threatened by deforestation, development, climate change, and pollution. The nation's shrimp and fishing industry is directly tied to the health of its mangrove forests, which serve as the nurseries for shrimp and fish. Besides sheltering these marine animals, the mangroves provide habitat for birds and protect coastal areas from storms. Many of Pakistan's mangrove forests have been lost, mostly due to the diversion of freshwater upstream for agricultural irrigation.

Pakistan's greatest environmental threat is its population. As it struggles to meet the needs of its 187 million people, the nation is experiencing habitat degradation caused by multiple sources: deforestation,

DEOSAI NATIONAL PARK

Located on the second-highest plateau in the world, Deosai National Park has an average elevation of 13,500 feet (4,115 m). This 1,158-square-mile (3,000-sq-km) park is home to brown bears, snow leopards, ibexes, urials, golden marmots, wolves, and foxes.[5] Golden eagles, lammageier and griffon vultures, laggar and peregrine falcons, and Himalayan snowcocks can all be found there as well. Deosai National Park is snowbound from November to May. But in the spring, the air is filled with butterflies and the park is carpeted with millions of wildflowers, stretching across miles of open rocky plain and stopping only at the edge of Sheosar Lake or the slopes of distant mountains. Nanga Parbat, the ninth-highest mountain in the world, is visible from parts of Deosai.

desertification, overuse, erosion, industrial pollution, agricultural runoff, wetland destruction, sewage, illegal hunting, and development. Additionally, practices such as trade in wildlife body parts are threatening certain animals. These practices are hard to control when a substance such as musk from the musk deer can be worth more than $20,000 per pound ($45,000 per kg).[6]

A huge source of pollution is Pakistan's leather industry. Leather goods are Pakistan's second-largest export after textiles. Pakistan's leather industry has factories in many cities, including Karachi, Sailkot, Lahore, Multan, Gujranwala, and Kasur.

Kasur, located east of Lahore in Punjab Province, is world famous for its environmental crisis. It is the site of one-third of Pakistan's tannery industry, which produces leather from sheep, buffalo, goats, and cows. Pollution in Kasur is some of the worst in the world. The groundwater and surrounding lands are contaminated with toxic chemicals, including mercury, copper, cadmium, lead, and chromium. Toxins, including heavy metals, are also carried in irrigation waters and absorbed by crops. Kasur residents suffer from diseases directly related to air and water pollution, facing high rates of diarrhea, dysentery, respiratory problems, and skin conditions. In 2005, Kasur's Civil Society Network published a report indicating that 70 percent of the diseases in the area were environmentally connected.[7]

Pakistan is home to 21 endangered and nine critically endangered species.

Kasur's water treatment plant is not enough to prevent water pollution from the town's tanneries.

Working with the United Nations Development Programme, the Punjab provincial government began the Kasur Tanneries Pollution Control Project in 1996. Although the project constructed a large water treatment plant to treat runoff, pollution levels remain critically high in the community.

CONSERVATION EFFORTS

Across Pakistan, 24 areas have been declared national parks, and all of them provide valuable habitat for Pakistan's embattled wildlife. Some parks were designated to protect particular species, others were chosen to retain unique landscapes, and a few were set aside for recreation.

Pakistan has participated in three United Nations (UN) conventions that have encouraged protection of the nation's environment and wildlife. Those conventions include the UN's Convention on Biological Diversity, the Convention of Climate Change, and the Convention on Combating Desertification. Some of the requirements of these conventions have been fulfilled by protecting areas such as national parks. Doing so protects diversity and habitat for plants and animals, in addition to safeguarding the soil, water, and air.

Pakistan has 14 national parks.

One of Pakistan's largest and highest national parks is Khunjerab National Park in Gilgit Baltistan, which covers approximately 876 square miles (2,270 sq km). Lying next to this park

is China's Taxkorgan Natural Reserve, which covers 5,405 square miles (14,000 sq km).[8] With help from the World Wildlife Fund (WWF), UN Development Programme (UNDP), Aga Khan Development Network (AKDN), and the International Center for Integrated Mountain Development (ICIMOD), officials of Gilgit Baltistan, Pakistan's Ministry of Environment, and China met to discuss natural reserves and socioeconomic issues for communities in the area. The long-term goal of this collaboration is to establish an international peace park.

Khunjerab National Park is on the Chinese border.

CHAPTER 4

HISTORY: STRIVING FOR STABILITY

Human habitation in Pakistan stretches back into the distant Paleolithic period. Two-million-year-old stone artifacts have been found in the Pabbi Hills. Other artifacts have been traced to the early Middle Paleolithic period, with stone hand axes from the Rohri Hills dating back 500,000 years or more. In addition, there is evidence that 45,000 years ago, people lived in open-air structures in the Soan River valley, rather than in caves or rock shelters. Mehrgarh, a Neolithic site in present-day Balochistan, shows evidence of mud brick structures and early agriculture, including domesticated barley dating back 9,000 years.

The people of Mehrgarh grew and stored crops, raised animals, made baskets, and created copper tools.

Pakistan's first major civilization built the city of Mohenjo Daro.

INDUS RIVER VALLEY

The culture of the Indus River valley flourished 4,500 years ago, at the same time as the better-known cultures of Egypt and Mesopotamia. Spreading from the foothills of the Himalayas to the Arabian Sea, this early culture covered an area larger than present-day Pakistan and was the largest of the three ancient cultures. The Indus valley people apparently traded with both the Egyptians and the Mesopotamians, as Indus artifacts have been found at sites in Egypt and Sumer. Two major urban centers of this culture were Harappa in Punjab Province and Mohenjo Daro in Sindh Province.

Yet the Indus River valley culture remains a bit of a mystery. In excavating sites in the Indus valley, archaeologists found no evidence of an obvious central government, no temples to indicate religious worship, and nothing to suggest a system of royalty. Evidence was discovered, however, that these people fired pottery, made earthenware figurines, manufactured beads, and worked gold and copper. The Indus valley culture had paved roads, multistory buildings constructed of fired clay bricks, and a water management system that included drains and sewers. The Indus people kept dogs, cats, camels, goats, sheep, and cattle, and they grew crops, including barley and wheat.

Regardless, the Indus River valley culture disappeared in approximately 1,900 BCE. And even though it left behind objects such as seals and tablets, they were written in a script that is undecipherable today.

CONTROLLED BY OUTSIDERS

In approximately 500 BCE, Buddhism spread across northern India and the Indus River valley. The archaeological site at Taxila, located outside Rawalpindi, was once the capital of Gandhara, a historical region and a crossroads for international trade that was ruled by various groups. Founded around 600 BCE, Taxila was a center of Buddhist teaching as early as 400 BCE and remained so for many centuries. Today, because of its cultural importance, Taxila is recognized by the United Nations Educational, Scientific, and Cultural Organization as a UNESCO World Heritage site.

In 326 BCE, Alexander III of Macedonia, called "the Great," crossed the Indus River near present-day Attock in northern Punjab. After his conquests, Greek rule in one form or another lasted into the first century CE. Around this time, the Kushan Empire expanded across

Clay seal from Mohenjo Daro

GANDHARAN ART

Sculptures of the Buddha in human form, either standing or sitting, are hallmarks of Gandharan art. Carved in a hillside, on a frieze, or as freestanding statues, these carvings flourished in stupas and monasteries across northern Pakistan. Some very large, carved, stone statues of the Buddha still exist in parts of Pakistan. Unfortunately, some of the Buddhas are under threat by Muslim fundamentalists, who consider the ancient statues blasphemous and wish to destroy them.

Pakistan into northern India, ruling until its decline in 250 CE. In addition, the Gupta Empire in India expanded into present-day Sindh Province. Much of the rest of Pakistan was broken into independent states, some of which were remnants of Kushan holdings.

Islam was brought to Pakistan early in the eighth century CE, when Mohammad bin Qasim invaded Sindh. After the eleventh century, conversion to Islam became widespread across Pakistan and northern India as the region fell under Turkish control for several centuries. The Mughal Empire out of India became prominent in the early sixteenth century. The Mughals remained in power approximately 200 years, until the death of Emperor Aurangzeb in 1707. With his death, the Mughal Empire quickly declined, although it did not completely disappear until after 1857.

Aurangzeb built the Badshahi Mosque in Lahore.

Taking advantage of this decline, the Sikhs began a push to power. They established their first stronghold in Gujranwala under Chait Singh, grandfather of the Sikh's greatest ruler, Ranjit Singh. Ranjit Singh seized Lahore in 1799, and shortly after this success, he declared himself maharaja, or prince, of Punjab. He subdued other Sikh and Pashtun kingdoms, uniting all of Punjab under his rule.

Also during this period, the British East India Company, a trading company, was taking control of much of the rest of the Indian subcontinent. Ranjit Singh died in Lahore on June 27, 1839, and within six years, Punjab had been torn apart by rival factions. By the end of the 1850s, the British ruled the subcontinent, including most of Pakistan.

Even under British rule, there was tension between the region's Muslims and Hindus. When the India National Congress was formed in 1885 to work toward Indian independence, Muslim members felt outnumbered and disregarded by the Hindu majority. To balance the India National Congress, the All India Muslim League was formed in 1906. Mohammed Ali Jinnah joined the league in 1913, and was soon recognized as a leader of the movement. At first, Jinnah wanted to preserve Indian unity, but he worried that Islamic interests would be ignored by the Hindu majority. Eventually, he came to believe that a separate Islamic nation was necessary to protect members of his faith on the Indian subcontinent. His work was instrumental in bringing about an independent Islamic state, causing him to be known as the father of Pakistan.

AN INDEPENDENT PAKISTAN

On August 14, 1947, at the time of Indian independence, the United Kingdom divided its former territory into a predominately Hindu India and a predominately Islamic Pakistan. At the time of partition, Pakistan was much larger than it is today, and it consisted of two sections: West Pakistan and East Pakistan. The two sections of the country were separated by 1,000 miles (1,600 km), the width of India. Jinnah became the first governor-general, the head of state. Although the government was technically led by a prime minister and a parliament, Jinnah wielded the most power in the new country.

The situation in the newly created country was desperate. Millions of refugees fled between the two countries, with Hindus leaving Pakistan for India and Muslims leaving India for Pakistan. India maintained control over the greater share of the resources of the old British India, including the military, the treasury, and most of the industry. The two countries quickly

MOHAMMED ALI JINNAH

Mohammed Ali Jinnah was born in Karachi on December 25, 1876. He was educated there as a child, but at the age of 16, he was sent to Great Britain to become a lawyer. He attended the All India National Congress in Calcutta in 1906 and joined the All India Muslim League in 1913. He united India's Muslims and eventually established Pakistan as a home for them. After being sworn in as governor-general on August 14, 1947, Jinnah served as the first leader of the newly formed Pakistan. He died in Karachi on September 11, 1948, after suffering a lengthy illness.

became enemies, fighting over boundaries and the distribution of resources. Worst of all for Pakistan, India controlled the sources of Pakistan's major rivers, meaning the larger country could potentially block the smaller country's water supply. Many international experts predicted that Pakistan would quickly disintegrate and be annexed by India.

Thirteen months after the creation of Pakistan, on September 11, 1948, Jinnah died of tuberculosis. Three years later, on October 16, 1951, Pakistan's first prime minister, Liaquat Ali Khan, was assassinated in Rawalpindi. Liaquat had wanted to create a constitution for the new nation, but he died while the many competing factions were still struggling to reach agreement.

A constitution was finally approved in 1956. Under the new constitution, the position of governor-general was converted to president. The constitution called for the government to be controlled by a parliament, called the National Assembly, and a prime minister. However, the president, Iskander Mirza, who had been the last governor-general, continued to dominate. As chaos continued in the national government, in the provinces, and between the country's religious groups, Mirza nullified the constitution in 1958. He declared martial law and appointed a general, Mohammad Ayub Khan, as chief administrator.

> **Liaquat Ali Khan was also called *qaid-i-millet*, or "leader of the country."**

Mohammed Ali Jinnah in 1947, one day after Pakistan achieved independence

Within a month, Ayub Khan staged a coup, taking over the government and arresting Mirza. Mirza was then exiled from the country.

MILITARY RULE

Instead of allowing full democracy and reinstating a parliament, Ayub Khan called for the creation of so-called basic democracies, which allowed people to make local decisions. Under Ayub Khan's regime, the economy grew, in part because of aid from the United States. However, the gains were concentrated in West Pakistan. Although the East Pakistanis outnumbered the West Pakistanis, they were beginning to feel marginalized and separate from the rest of the country. In general, they also disapproved of Ayub Khan's coup.

Mohammad Ayub Khan served in the Indian army before the partition.

Ayub Khan won an election in January 1965, but voting was open only to members of basic democracies. The following summer, Ayub Khan led the country during another conflict with India, a skirmish over Kashmir. Because of losses suffered in this conflict, Ayub Khan's power and prestige diminished. Ayub Khan retired in 1969, choosing another general, Agha Mohammad Yahya Khan, as his successor.

An election was scheduled for 1970. The new election was intended to pass power from the president back to the prime minister and the parliament. When the votes were tallied, East Pakistan's Mujibur Rahman, called Mujib, and his Awami League had the most seats in the National

Assembly. Zulfikar Ali Bhutto and the Pakistan People's Party (PPP) of West Pakistan had half as many seats. Yet Bhutto refused to accept the election results, arguing that no West Pakistan provinces had voted for Mujib.

Unable to resolve the conflict, Yahya Khan declared on March 1 that the nation's system of government would have to be altered. Mujib and the people of East Pakistan were outraged. Strikes and mass demonstrations began, and on March 25, Yahya Khan called in the army to stop the protests. A bloody conflict enveloped East Pakistan, drawing India into the fray. On December 16, 1971, the conflict ended—West Pakistan lost and East Pakistan formally became a separate country, Bangladesh, soon thereafter. After the humiliating loss, Yahya Khan turned the government over to Bhutto, who served as president from 1971 to 1973.

Pakistan returned to a democratic government for a short time after the conflict over East Pakistan. Bhutto became prime minister in 1973 when a new constitution was enacted. However, Bhutto consolidated his power and created a paramilitary organization for his personal protection called the Federal Security Force (FSF). He also began imprisoning and silencing his critics.

A general election was held in March 1977—the first election held under civilian rule since the partition 30 years earlier. Nine opposition parties united to run against Bhutto, but Bhutto and his PPP won 155 of the 200 seats in the National Assembly. The opposition accused the PPP of rigging the election, and demonstrations erupted. General Mohammad

MADRASSA

A madrassa is a religious school that teaches reading and religion. It trains mullahs, or people educated in Islamic theology and law. Madrassas have a long history, and many children from poor families attend them as a way to get a minimal education. Madrassas did not traditionally teach fanaticism or violence.

Zia-ul-Haq seized control in a coup and became president. He had Bhutto hanged in 1979.

In December 1979, the Soviet Union invaded Afghanistan. Initially, Afghan tribes rallied their own fighters to battle the Soviets. In an effort to raise fighters, the war was presented as a jihad, or a religious struggle, drawing Muslims to the cause. The United States, Arab allies, and European nations poured billions of dollars into the fight against the Soviets. The money was mostly channeled through Zia and Pakistan's military.

Soon, a group of Muslim guerrillas called the mujahideen, a word meaning "strugglers" or "people doing jihad," became prominent in the conflict. And the fighting in Afghanistan became a religious war, rather than one for the people's freedom. Saudi-funded madrassas in western Pakistan began teaching Wahhabism, a conservative, intolerant style of

Zulfikar Ali Bhutto rallied his supporters in 1969.

Islam. They also began recruiting and training guerrilla fighters to drive the Soviets out of Afghanistan, receiving covert support from the United States.

Meanwhile, Zia was reorganizing the Pakistani political system along Islamic lines. A vote in 1984 confirmed that the majority approved of the country's Islamic direction, although voter turnout was low. Zia chose his prime minister, Muhammad Khan Junejo. When martial law was lifted in 1985, Benazir Bhutto—daughter of Zulfikar Ali Bhutto and leader of the PPP—emerged as Junejo's chief political rival. Amid major turmoil in 1988, Zia dissolved Junejo's government and promised to hold a new election. Before this could happen, however, Zia died in an airplane explosion on August 17.

CONTINUING STRUGGLES

Under the existing laws for the succession of leaders, Ghulam Ishaq Khan, a legislator, became president, and in the 1988 election, Benazir Bhutto became prime minister. Her government was dismissed two years later, as Bhutto lost support and became unable to govern. Her rival, Nawaz Sharif, became prime minister. Ishaq Khan gained more power during this time, however.

Ishaq Khan soon used his power to dissolve Sharif's government in 1993, claiming that Sharif was unable to govern. Sharif protested to the nation's supreme court, which took his side. At this point, the military stepped in and convinced both men to resign their positions. The military invited Moeen Qureshi, a businessman who had been living in New York City, to head an interim government. Qureshi took major steps toward ending corruption and resolving Pakistan's social and economic problems.

In the next national election, held in October 1993, Bhutto regained the office of prime minister. However, scandal enveloped her again, and the country spiraled out of control. Ethnic conflict erupted in Karachi, and tribes in several regions pushed for greater independence. Drug and weapons dealers took advantage of the chaos. Bhutto's government was dissolved in November 1996, and in the next election, held in 1997, Sharif

BENAZIR BHUTTO

Benazir Bhutto became politically active to raise support for her father's release from prison, but she was arrested repeatedly for her activities and spent much of the time from 1979 to 1984 under house arrest. In January 1984, General Zia allowed her to travel to London for medical reasons. She remained in England until 1986, when she returned to Pakistan to campaign for Zia's resignation.

When a free election was held in 1988, the PPP won a sweeping victory. Benazir Bhutto became prime minister of Pakistan on December 1, 1988. She was the first female head of government democratically elected in an Islamic country and one of the youngest heads of state in the world. As prime minister, Bhutto, along with her husband Asif Ali Zardari, faced accusations of corruption. She and her government were dismissed in August 1990 by President Ghulam Ishaq Khan. Reelected in 1993, Bhutto was again dismissed on corruption charges by President Farooq Leghari.

Bhutto left Pakistan in 1999 and lived abroad until October 18, 2007. Within hours of her return to Pakistan, a suicide bomber made an attempt on her life. She was assassinated on December 27, 2007, in Rawalpindi.

regained office. Under Sharif, Pakistan tested nuclear weapons, straining the country's relations with the United States and many other countries.

Sharif failed to control the country, however, and on October 12, 1999, the military dissolved his government. General Pervez Musharraf gained control in the coup, but he kept the constitution in effect and did not declare martial law. He did suspend the legislature, however, and take full power for himself. After the September 11, 2001, terrorist attacks on New York City and Washington DC prompted the United States to invade Afghanistan, Musharraf allied Pakistan with the United States. This alliance angered Muslim conservatives, whose sympathies lay with the Afghan Taliban, the religious-based government accused of hiding the terrorists.

Pervez Musharraf's family moved from India to Pakistan at the time of partition when he was four.

As Pakistan stabilized, political opponents began demanding Musharraf return the country to civilian authority. Reacting to demonstrations and a battle in the nation's supreme court, Musharraf stepped down as head of the military in 2007 but retained his post as president.

An election was scheduled for 2008, and in the fall of 2007, Sharif and Bhutto both began campaigning. In December, the nation was stunned when Bhutto was assassinated at a campaign stop. Bhutto's party won the most seats in parliament, and Yousaf Raza Gilani became prime minister.

Benazir Bhutto waves to supporters after the 1988 elections.

Members of the PPP remember Benazir Bhutto on the third anniversary of her death.

Musharraf resigned soon after, and Bhutto's widower, Asif Ali Zardari, assumed the presidency.

Strife continued in Pakistan. A 2010 flood left 1,500 dead and millions more hungry or homeless.[1] A religious fanatic assassinated the governor of Punjab, Salman Taseer, in January 2011. Looking ahead, the struggling nation seemed to have many problems to overcome.

CHAPTER 5

PEOPLE: TRIBAL TRADITIONS

The people of Pakistan are ethnically diverse due to the area's long history of invasions by outside groups. Today, Pakistanis can trace their family origins back to Dravidian, Indo-Aryan, Greek, Scythian, Hun, Arab, Mongol, Persian, and Afghan invasions or migrations. Pakistani ties are based mostly on family, language, and tribal group. Religion is important, but as the violent secession of East Pakistan in 1971 showed, religion is not a strong binding force. Today, Pakistan is being violently torn asunder again, and religion is not a tie but a wedge.

POPULATION GROWTH AND URBANIZATION

Pakistan is a very young country in a very old land. It has one of the world's highest rates of population growth, increasing from 32 million to

Religion is important in Pakistan.

DEMOGRAPHICS

Pakistan has a young population, with 35.4 percent under age 15 and only 4.2 percent over age 65. The median age is 21.6, and the sex ratio has remained fairly constant, with an average of 1.07 males for each female up to age 65. The life expectancy is 64.18 years for men and 67.9 years for women. The county's fertility rate is 3.17 children per woman.[4]

almost 200 million in its 64-year history.[1] In 2011, the nation's birthrate was 24.81 births per 1,000 residents, ranking it sixty-second in the world. Its population growth rate was 1.573 percent, seventy-fifth in the world.

Along with its booming population growth, Pakistan is changing rapidly from a rural society to an urban one. Although only 36 percent of the population lived in an urban area in 2010, the rate of urbanization was 3.1 percent per year. Karachi, Pakistan's largest city, has a population of more than 13 million, and the next three largest cities—Lahore, Faisalabad, and Rawalpindi—have a combined population of almost 12 million.[2] It is estimated that Pakistan will be the fourth-most-populous nation by 2050, behind China, India, and the United States.[3]

LANGUAGES AND ETHNIC GROUPS

The people of Pakistan follow many different cultural traditions and speak a wide variety of languages and dialects. Even though most Pakistanis belong to one of five major linguistic groups—Punjabi, Sindhi, Pashto, Urdu, and Balochi—they also speak one or more other languages,

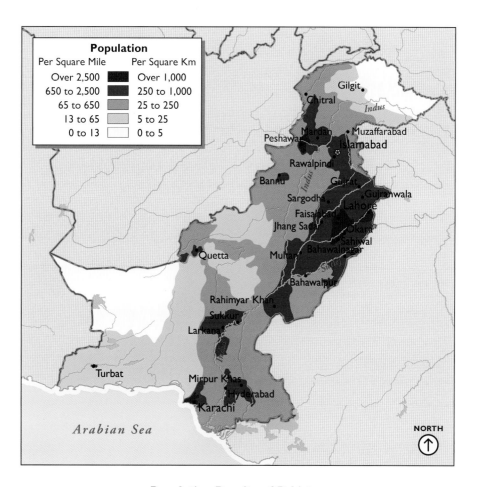

Population

Per Square Mile	Per Square Km
Over 2,500	Over 1,000
650 to 2,500	250 to 1,000
65 to 650	25 to 250
13 to 65	5 to 25
0 to 13	0 to 5

Gilgit

Chitral

Indus

Mardan • Muzaffarabad

Peshawar Islamabad

Rawalpindi

Bannu *Indus* Gujrat

Gujranwala

Sargodha Lahore

Faisalabad

Jhang Sadr Okara

Sahiwal

Bahawalnagar

Quetta Multan

Bahawalpur

Rahimyar Khan

Sukkur

Larkana

Turbat

Mirpur Khas

Hyderabad

Karachi

Arabian Sea

NORTH
↑

Population Density of Pakistan

generally including English. Across northern Pakistan, a number of local languages are spoken by varying numbers of people. For example, in Gilgit Baltistan, people speak Shina, Burushaki, Wakhi, Khowari, or Balti, in addition to the official languages of Urdu and English. In Azad Kashmir, local languages include Kashmiri, Pahari, and Gujari. Seraikis live in Punjab, and the Seraiki language is a variation of Punjabi.

The three major ethnic groups in Pakistan are the Punjabi, the Pashtun, and the Sindhi. The Pashtun tribal tradition is one of honor

YOU SAY IT!

English	Urdu	Pashto
Hello	Salam (sah-lahm)	As-salaamu' alaykum (ahs-sah-lah-moh ah-lay-koom)
Good morning	A salam alekum (ah sah-lahm a-lay-koom)	Sahar pikheyr (sah-hahr pihk-hair)
Good night	Shab ba kahir (shahb bah kah-heer)	Shpa mo pa kheyr (shuh-pah moh pah khair)
Thank you	shukriya (shuhk-ree-yah)	Manana (mah-nah-nah)

and revenge. The Pashtun are closely related to the Afghanis and traditionally more conservative in their Islamic beliefs than either the Punjabis or Sindhis. This is due, in great part, to the long history of influence from Sufi mystics in both Sindh and Punjab. Sufi saints conveyed Islamic principles and Koranic texts through teaching and their own spirituality, and they promoted harmony and peace through personal example.

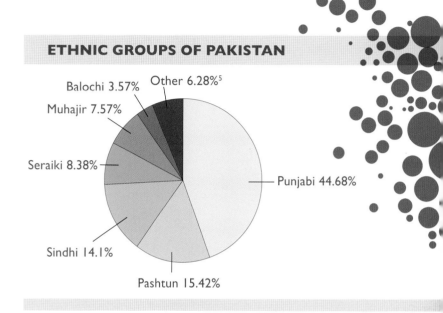

ETHNIC GROUPS OF PAKISTAN

- Balochi 3.57%
- Other 6.28%[5]
- Muhajir 7.57%
- Seraiki 8.38%
- Sindhi 14.1%
- Pashtun 15.42%
- Punjabi 44.68%

The people of Sindh were independent prior to British annexation in the nineteenth century. In 1937, they won back their autonomy from British rule but became part of Pakistan after independence. The Sindhis are a mix of Muslim and Hindu. With the influx of Muhajirs (Muslim refugees) from India at the time of the partition, the dynamics between Hindu and Muslim became violent in Sindh. The majority of the Hindu population—many of whom were merchants, government workers, teachers, and writers—fled Sindh. This flight by much of the professional and intellectual class left a vacuum in Sindh's cultural identity.

RELIGION

Islam, the major religion in Pakistan, crosses both ethnic and linguistic lines. Sunni Muslims make up 75 percent of the population, and Shia Muslims make up 20 percent.[6] The Sunnis and Shias are further divided into sects or schools, such as Deobandi and Barelvi. Sufism, a mystical movement within Islam, has had a strong influence in Pakistan as well.

The remaining 5 percent of Pakistan's population is made up of Christians, Hindus, Sikhs, Buddhists, and people of other religions, including a number of different minorities. Among the minorities in Pakistan are the Kalasha, also known as "Wearers of the Black Robes." The Kalasha live in a few valleys of the Hindu Kush near Chitral in the northwest, and they practice a completely different culture and religion. Kalasha women can choose their own husbands and even change husbands, if they wish. Some legends say they are descendents of Alexander the Great's army. They speak Kalasha and are not Muslim but nature-oriented polytheists who make animal sacrifices. They are considered a primitive pagan tribe by many Muslims and are referred to as the *Kafir Kalash*. *Kafir* means "unbeliever" or "infidel" in Urdu.

But polytheists are not the only Kafir group in Pakistan. Muslim fundamentalists do not recognize many religious groups, including other Islamic sects, as legitimate and classify them as infidels. One minority Islamic sect is the Ahmadiyyah, whose members are not recognized by

Visitors visit the shrine of a Sufi mystic in Lahore.

Kalash girl in traditional dress

Pakistani law as Muslims. A number of anti-Ahmadiyyah laws have been passed in the country. On May 28, 2010, Islamist extremist members of the Taliban attacked two Ahmadiyyah mosques in Lahore, killing 94 people and injuring more than 100.[7] Many fundamental Sunnis would also like to classify the Ismailites, a Shia sect, as non-Muslim.

TRIBAL LIFE

The Pashtun, also called Pakhtun or Pathans, of Khyber Pakhtunkhwa consist of a number of tribes and clans, including the Yusufzai, Khattaks, Wazirs, and Afridis. They all follow a strict code of behavior called Pakhtunwali. Found across far-western Pakistan, Pakhtunwali is based on several key principles, including honor, revenge, and hospitality. Rights and obligations are equally shared by members of tribes and subtribes. Tribes live in a small group setting or village, or they live in a scattered and extended joint-family system. An assembly of tribal elders called a *jirga* serves as the prominent institution for doing tribal business and resolving issues according to *riwaj*, or tradition. The Baloch and Brahui tribes of Balochistan are similar in makeup and beliefs.

The tribal system is also important in the Federally Administered Tribal Area (FATA). As an area never fully controlled by the British, it has maintained its autonomy since 1893 and the creation of the Durand Line, Pakistan's border with Afghanistan. Similar to the provinces of Khyber Pakhtunkhwa and Balochistan, FATA is filled with different tribal groups: Utmankhel, Mohmand, Tarkani, Safi, Afridi, Shilmani, Mulagori, Orakzai, Turi, Bangash, Masozai, Darwesh Khel Wazirs, Mahsuds, Utmanzai,

Ahmadzai, Bhittani, Wazir, Kharasin, and Shirani, among others. This semiautonomous collection of large and small tribes and subtribes also has a very strong tribal structure, and hospitality is a cornerstone of their cultures.

The tribes are governed by a jirga, which resolves local disputes. The jirga can also act like a court, handing out punishments for violations of local customs. For large disputes involving separate tribes in FATA, a jirga is convened with the head of the tribal agency; *maliks,* or tribal chiefs; and tribal elders. A malik receives a *mojib*, or allowance, from the tribal agency to help offset hospitality expenses required for jirgas. The people's respect for an individual malik is largely based on that man's weapons and the number of followers who wield them on his behalf.

Meeting of a Pashtun tribal jirga

CHAPTER 6
CULTURE:
A COLORFUL NATION

Breaking the culture barrier with someone from Pakistan might be as easy as asking him or her about sports—specifically, field hockey or cricket. Of Pakistan's ten Olympic medals, eight have been in field hockey, including three gold medals.[1] But Pakistanis' love for the game of cricket may be their greatest unifier. Across the country, from the streets of big cities to the dusty fields of rural areas, both men and boys play makeshift games of cricket.

Pakistan's national cricket team is rated among the best in the world, including the teams of the United Kingdom, Australia, India, Sri Lanka, and South Africa. Pakistan won the Cricket World Cup in 1992 and took the International Cricket Council (ICC) World Twenty20 in 2009. But Pakistan's internal problems have begun to interfere with the sport on the international level. After the November 2008 terrorist

Cricket is hugely popular in Pakistan.

attack in Mumbai, India severed its cricket ties with Pakistan. Shortly after this, in March 2009, a terrorist attack targeting the Sri Lankan cricket team in Lahore caused the ICC to ban Pakistan from hosting international games until the country's security problems are resolved. Since then, the Pakistan team has been involved with a series of gambling scandals, further damaging its image. In January 2011, however, the team won the 2010–2011 New Zealand Test Series, its first series win outside the subcontinent since 2003–2004. Another popular game among Pakistanis is snooker, a variation on billiards, and Pakistan's Billiards and Snooker Association competes internationally.

Pakistanis often have several names, including a name that indicates their job, status, or hometown.

CLOTHING

The most common traditional clothing worn throughout Pakistan by both men and women is called *shalwar-kamiz*. *Shalwar* are loose trousers, and a *kamiz* is a long, loose shirt that goes down to the knees. A woman's kamiz may have a large pocket in front. Women also wear a *dupatta*, a shawl or long piece of cloth used to cover the head and cascade over the shoulders.

Variations in dress are based on region or culture. Pakistanis in big cities often wear Western-style clothes. In some parts of the country,

Pakistani women often wear head scarves and colorful clothing.

MARRIAGE AND DIVORCE

Divorce is allowed in Pakistan, and women have a statutory right to end a marriage. Even so, Pakistan is a patriarchal country, and so the system works mostly in men's favor. Arranged marriages are still common, including child marriages. In some areas of Pakistan, so-called honor killings of women are a tradition. They frequently involve a woman who wants a divorce, who marries against her family's wishes, or who is in a sexual relationship with a man.

Among the Kalash people, a woman may choose her husband. She may also decide to leave her husband and do so fairly easily. In the tribal areas of FATA, however, women are required to be very submissive to men. In addition, men can have multiple wives.

turbans are common headwear for men, but a number of other caps and hats are worn, as well, including the *karakul*, which is shaped like a boat.

In FATA, women observe strict purdah from outsiders and wear a burka, leaving only their eyes uncovered. Men in FATA wear traditional clothes with a large turban, and they often carry their rifles on their shoulders. The Pashtun people of Khyber Pakhtunkhwa dress similarly, whereas their neighbors, the Kalash, distinguish themselves by their clothing. Kalash women wear an elaborate headdress with a long train covered with cowrie shells and other decorations. Kalash men wear a woolen hat decorated with feathers and bells.

MUSIC AND LITERATURE

Today, music is being banned in conservative areas of Pakistan, but music has had a long tradition throughout the country. Differences in traditional Pakistani music styles are generally based on rhythm and the style of poetry being sung. The best-known music in Pakistan is *qawwali*, a form of Sufi devotional music with a tradition going back 700 years. Although it is most popular in Punjab and Sindh, qawwali is quickly gaining an international following. Merging Sufi poetry styles, such as *ghazal* and *kafi*, with light classical and folk styles, today's qawwali singers might combine traditional instruments with the sounds of electric guitars, keyboards, and drums. Also popular is Hindustani classical music.

Some performers have become known outside Pakistan, including Pashtun singers such as Zarsanga, known for her folk songs; Khayal Muhammad, a singer of ghazals; and pop singer Rahim Shah. Qawwali singers today include Rahat Fateh Ali Kahn, who sings mostly in Punjabi

TRADITIONAL INSTRUMENTS

Traditional instruments include drums such as the *tabla*, *dholak*, and *naghara*. Stringed instruments include the three-stringed *tumba*, the *sarangi*, and the *sitar*. Flutes made of bamboo or reed are also played.

Small, portable boxlike harmoniums became common after being introduced in the late 1800s. Somewhat like an organ, the harmonium opens in the back to allow the musician to work a bellows. Typically, the musician works the bellows with the left hand and plays the keyboard with the right hand.

Man with a traditional drum, Lahore

and is known for his folk songs. The music of Arif Lohar is considered representative of the traditional folk heritage of Punjab.

Music is also an important element of festivals and gatherings. The Pashtun's Khattak tribe performs twirling acrobatic feats with swords, accompanied by pounding drums that keep the beat. The Kalash are known for their vibrant and enthusiastic music and dance. Their largest festival, Choimus, involves three weeks of singing, dancing, and feasting each December.

Pakistan also has a rich tradition of literature, especially poetry. Today, the Pashtuns revere Khushhal Khan Khatak (1613–1689). A chief of the Khatak tribe, he is admired for his warrior skills but remembered for his writings. He authored some 350 works of poetry and prose on topics ranging from religion, ethics, philosophy, and medicine to sports. A contemporary was the renowned poet Abdur Rahman (1650–1715), who is venerated as a Sufi mystic and whose works show a Persian influence.

Western music is slowly coming to Pakistan; two rock groups include Vital Signs and Junoon.

Muhammad Iqbal (1877–1938) is considered the national poet of Pakistan. He is recognized for his work toward establishing an independent Islamic state, although he died a decade before Pakistan came into being. His birthday is celebrated as a national holiday.

Today, several Pakistani novelists are becoming prominent internationally. Mohsin Hamid was a finalist for a PEN/Hemingway Award and won a Betty Trask Award for his book *Moth Smoke*, published in 2000. The book was also selected as a New York Times Notable Book of the Year and adapted for a television miniseries in Pakistan. Hamid's second book, *The Reluctant Fundamentalist*, published in 2007, was a runner-up for a Man Booker Prize for Fiction.

HOLIDAYS AND RELIGIOUS OBSERVANCES

March 23: Pakistan Day, which commemorates the 1940 Lahore Resolution, the political statement that called for Islamic autonomy in India.

August 14: Independence Day

November 9: Muhammad Iqbal's birthday

December 25: Mohammed Ali Jinnah's birthday

The dates of Islamic religious holidays vary each year, as they are based on a lunar calendar. Observances of the following holidays also vary between Sunni and Shia Muslims:

Eid-ul-Adha (Festival of Sacrifice): In fall, often November

Eid-ul-Fitr (end of Ramadan): Late August, or 40 decades, the start of Ramadan

Eid-Milad-un-Nabi (birth of the prophet): February

Ashura (commemoration of Husayn ibn Ali): December

LOLLYWOOD

Based in Lahore, the Pakistani film industry is called Lollywood. What was generally considered the industry's golden age ended approximately 40 years ago, and over the last decades, many Pakistani films have followed tired clichés. A number of Pakistani actors have gone to India's Bollywood to find work. Lately, independent filmmakers have been moving the Pakistani film industry forward.

Sabiha Sumar's 2003 film *Khamosh Pani* (*Silent Waters*) won a Golden Leopard award at the Locarno International Film Festival in Switzerland. Sumar has also won acclaim for her documentary films dealing with Pakistani social issues. Her 2006 film *For a Place under the Heavens* follows how each government in Pakistan's history has contributed to the rise of fundamentalism, and her 2008 film *Dinner with the President: A Nation's Journey* was featured on PBS's program *Independent Lens.* Shoaib Mansoor's 2007 film *Khuda Kai Liye* (*In the Name of God*) was considered a success in Pakistan and in India.

FOOD

Pakistani's eat wheat, rice, and meats in a variety of dishes with different spices. In Punjab, spicy curries and sauces predominate, while in northwestern Pakistan, foods tend to be more bland. In Sindh, fish is eaten more than anywhere else in the country. Rice is a basic food, and dal, a mixture of lentils or beans, is common as well.

Pakistanis eat a lot of meat. However, pork is forbidden to Muslims. In western Pakistan, lamb is a staple, whether barbecued whole in Balochistan or cubed and made into kebabs in Khyber Pakhtunkhwa. Meat and vegetables may be cooked with cream or yogurt, and meat may be

Many Pakistanis eat sitting on the floor around a short table; many also eat without utensils.

Some rural women still make chapati the traditional way,
on an outdoor mud stove.

ground, mixed with vegetables and spices, and cooked as kebabs. There are many ways to make most Pakistani dishes, and ingredients vary greatly.

Meals are accompanied with bread, usually flatbread. In Pakistan, types include unleavened breads, such as chapati, roti, puri, and paratha. Naan is a leavened flatbread. Tea, called chai, is the usual beverage. Because Pakistan is an Islamic country, the consumption of alcohol is forbidden.

ART AND CRAFTS

Lahore may consider itself the heart of Pakistan's art and culture, but Khyber Pakhtunkhwa claims to have originated Pakistan's pop art movement. There, artists paint every inch of surface on a vehicle, both inside and out, making something known as truck art. They use bright enamel colors to depict floral designs, folk motifs, and portraits of politicians and movie

ARCHITECTURE

Monumental architecture in Pakistan dates back to the stupa mound at Mohenjo Daro from the third millennium BCE and to the Great Stupa at Taxila, begun in the first century BCE. Mosques have existed since Islam was introduced to the region in the eighth century CE. Pearl Mosque in Lahore was built in the seventeenth century by Shah Jahan, who also built the famous Taj Mahal in India. The Badshahi Mosque, also in Lahore, was commissioned by Aurangzeb, last of the Mughal emperors. The modern Faisal Mosque in Islamabad, completed in 1986, was inspired by a traditional tent and serves as Pakistan's national mosque.

stars. In creating three-dimensional effects, artists might affix wood, metal, or plastic in a collage. They often finish their work with calligraphy that presents a quote, poem, or slogan.

More traditional crafts include pottery, jewelry, hand-knotted carpets, and handwoven cloth. Weaving goes back to the days of Mohenjo Daro 4,500 years ago, and carpets from Lahore have been famous since at least the sixteenth century. Geometric and curvilinear patterns, leaf and floral designs, and realistic village and hunting scenes can be found on hand-knotted carpets from Pakistan. Metal work, particularly in brass, is both decorative and functional. Local artists are present at most markets in Pakistan selling their work.

Traditional embroidery on clothing and caps can be elaborate, incorporating beads, buttons, mirrors, and cowrie shells. Embroidery styles also involve different motifs and stitches. One complex interlaced stitch called *hurmitch* is used only in Sindh, whereas stitches such as cross, chain, and satin are common across traditions. Phulkari-style embroidery consists of colorful flower patterns in geometric designs or scenes of village life, depending on whether the embroiderer is Muslim or Hindu.

Wool is commonly used for clothing and embroidery in Sindh, Kashmir, and the area around Chitral. Cotton and silk are both widely used both for background fabric and for thread.

Art bus

CHAPTER 7
POLITICS: DEMOCRATIC IDEALS

Pakistan is an on-again, off-again democracy that has alternated between autocracy and oligarchy. Today, the dominant group is referred to as the Establishment, and it includes a collection of wealthy landowners, business tycoons, senior military officers, and key members of the judiciary. A democratically elected leader must abide by the

Pakistan flag

THE FLAG OF PAKISTAN

The flag of Pakistan has a green background and a white stripe running vertically down its left side. The stripe symbolizes the nation's religious minorities. In the center of the flag, over the green background, are a white crescent and star, both symbols of Islam.

wishes of the Establishment, or as history has shown, he or she will be quickly replaced.

Pakistan is a federal republic and divided into four provinces: Balochistan, Sindh, Punjab, and Khyber Pakhtunkhwa (formerly the North-West Frontier Province). The provinces are further divided into districts. Each province has its own assembly. The provincial assemblies make provincial laws and also help select the president of Pakistan.

Additionally, Pakistan includes FATA and a small area around the capital known as the Islamabad Capital Territory. Pakistan also administers two parts of the disputed Kashmir region: Azad Kashmir and Gilgit Baltistan. Both the northern area of Gilgit Baltistan and FATA are semiautonomous.

ORGANIZATION OF GOVERNMENT

In Pakistan, the legislative branch is made up of a bicameral parliament called the Majlis-e-Shoora. It consists of the Senate (upper house), with 100 seats, and the National Assembly (lower house), currently with 342 seats. Members of the National Assembly are elected by universal adult suffrage, which in Pakistan means that anyone over 18 years of age can vote. Members of the Senate are elected by the members of their respective provincial assemblies. Only the National Assembly can pass laws related to finance and approve the federal budget.

STRUCTURE OF THE GOVERNMENT OF PAKISTAN

Executive	Legislative	Judicial
President (head of state) Prime Minister (head of government)	Majlis-e-Shoora Upper House: Senate Lower House: National Assembly provincial assemblies	Supreme Court Federal Shariat provincial high courts district lower courts

The executive branch consists of a president and prime minister. Pakistan's president is elected by an electoral college comprised of the members of the Senate, the National Assembly, and the provincial assemblies. The president is elected to a five-year term, and he or she serves as the head of state. Pakistan's constitution requires that the president be a Muslim. The president can prevent passage of bills, unless both houses vote to overrule him or her. In 2011, the president was Asif Ali Zardari, elected in 2008.

The prime minister is chosen by the party that holds a majority in the parliament. The prime minister serves as the head of government and has a cabinet, or council of ministers, to assist him or her. These ministers are appointed by the president in consultation with the prime minister. If the prime minister loses his or her majority in parliament, the opposition

can force the sitting government out of office. In 2011, the prime minister was Syed Yousuf Gilani, appointed in 2008.

The judicial branch is independent from the rest of the government. The Supreme Court is the highest court in the land. It hears final appeals and has the power to judge government actions and laws unconstitutional. Each province has its own high court, and lower courts in the districts hear basic cases. The Federal Shariat, a court of Islamic law, ensures that new laws concur with the tenets of Islam.

STRIVING FOR DEMOCRACY

The rule of elected officials in Pakistan has been interrupted periodically by military takeovers. In fact, the military has ruled the country for more than half its existence. Despite these disruptions, the country keeps trying to retain its democratic ideals, even when it seems to be unable to define them.

On August 11, 1947, just days before the official creation of Pakistan, Mohammed Ali Jinnah, spoke to the Constituent Assembly of Pakistan in Karachi. In that speech, he stated:

Islamic law is called Sharia.

Prime Minister Syed Yousuf Gilani

You are free; you are free to go to your temples, you are free to go to your mosques or any other place of worship in this State of Pakistan. You may belong to any religion, caste or creed—that has nothing to do with the business of the state. . . . In course of time Hindus would cease to be Hindus and Muslims would cease to be Muslims—not in a religious sense, because that is the personal faith of an individual, but in a political sense as citizens of one State.[1]

RELIGIOUS FREEDOM

Jinnah's ideas on religious freedom as expressed in his August 14, 1947, speech were overruled by a number of constitutional requirements and laws. Today, holding office has religious requirements, and one group, the Ahmadiyyah, has been legally declared non-Muslim in Article 260.3 of Pakistan's constitution. This ruling prevents Ahmadis from holding the office of president. Under the rule of General Muhammad Zia-ul-Haq, Ahmadis could be imprisoned for publicly preaching or calling themselves Muslims.

Jinnah's statement surprised many people, considering that the overriding idea for the creation of Pakistan was that Muslims and Hindus could not live together. Yet the statement indicated that Jinnah realized the need for tolerance in the successful creation of a state. Unfortunately, Jinnah died the following year, and what he had in mind for the future of the country is unclear. Many subsequent Pakistani leaders have not been as open to other cultures and tolerant of other religions, however.

Women in Karachi hold up their voter ID cards, 2010.
Pakistan is working to become more democratic.

A CONSTANTLY CHANGING CONSTITUTION

On March 12, 1949, the Constituent Assembly passed the Objectives Resolution, which provided the foundation for Pakistan's constitution. Mostly moderate, the members of the assembly were not trying to create an Islamic theocracy. The Objectives Resolution included provisions for non-Muslims to freely follow their own religions and cultural practices and safeguarded their legitimate interests. The resolution made it clear that the Pakistanis were experimenting in creating a truly democratic Islamic state. Included in the resolution were statements such as "Sovereignty over the entire universe belongs to Almighty Allah alone" and "Principles of Democracy, freedom, equality, tolerance and social justice as enunciated by Islam shall be fully observed."[2]

> **Ten seats in the National Assembly are reserved for non-Muslims and 60 for women.**

The Objectives Resolution left open many issues, such as the division of power between the prime minister and the governor-general and the authority of the central government versus the provinces. In 1951, the assassination of Jinnah's prime minister and close confidant, Liaquat Ali Khan, made it unlikely these issues would be resolved. Since that time, the balance of power has fluctuated between the prime minister and the governor-general or president.

Pakistan adopted its first constitution on March 23, 1956. Establishing the nation as the Islamic Republic of Pakistan, it called for a parliamentary form of government and established a National Assembly

لا إله إلا الله محمد رسول الله

Parliament, Islamabad

to replace the Constituent Assembly. In addition, the office of president replaced that of governor general.

On October 7, 1958, President Iskander Mirza nullified the constitution. Twenty days later, he was removed from office by a coup led by the military's General Mohammad Ayub Khan. Ayub Khan declared himself president and issued a new constitution in early 1962. On March 25, 1969, martial law was imposed, the constitution was set aside, and General Agha Mohammad Yahya Khan took over. He led the push toward the Islamization of Pakistan.

Pakistan's current constitution was put in place on April 12, 1973. It restored the bicameral legislature and the position of prime minister as head of government. The 1973 constitution has been suspended three times since being instituted, the first time on July 5, 1977. It was restored on December 30, 1985, but then suspended again on October 15, 1999. It was restored in stages in 2002. On December 31, 2003, the constitution was amended. It was suspended again on November 3, 2007, but soon restored on December 15, 2007. On April 19, 2010, Zardari signed into law an amendment decreasing the power of the president to its intended ceremonial role, rolling back changes made by former president Pervez Musharraf that had increased presidential power.

Pakistan president Asif Ali Zardari, husband of the late Benazir Bhutto, met with flood victims in August 2010.

POLITICAL PARTIES

The current ruling party is the PPP, founded in 1967 by Zulfikar Ali Bhutto. PPP members currently hold the positions of both president and prime minister. The PPP by itself does not have enough members in the National Assembly to keep the current government in office. This means it has had to form a coalition with other parties to obtain the required majority. The ruling coalition consists of the PPP, the Muttahida Qaumi Movement (MQM), the Jamiat Ulema-i Islam Fazl-ur Rehman (JUI-F), the Awami National Party (ANP), five members from the Pakistan Muslim League–Functional (PML-F), and 17 independent members, though membership changes often.

FOREIGN RELATIONS

In part stemming from its internal instability, Pakistan has tense relationships with various other countries. Pakistan and India have remained hostile much of the time since the countries' partition, and the two continue to dispute their boundaries. In 2010, the nations resumed a dialogue, taking steps to improve their relations.

Pakistan displeased international allies such as the United States in the 1990s when it began testing nuclear weapons, causing the United States and others to stop giving Pakistan money for its military. After the September 11, 2001, terror attacks on New York and Washington DC, Pakistan became a key US ally in the global fight against terrorism because of its strategic location next to Afghanistan, where members of the al-Qaeda terrorist group were presumed to be hiding. The United States and others began supplying Pakistan's military once again. Since September 11, 2001, Pakistani forces have captured at least 600 members of al-Qaeda or other terrorist groups.[3]

On May 2, 2011, US forces killed al-Qaeda leader Osama bin Laden, who was living in a compound in Abbottabad, outside Islamabad. The operation strained relations between the countries. The United States worried that Pakistanis had been helping bin Laden, although there was no evidence that the government of Pakistan knew bin Laden's whereabouts. Pakistan's leaders believed they should have been warned about the US attack in advance and resented US intrusion on their soil. However, later in May 2011, both governments reaffirmed their partnership to fight al-Qaeda and other instigators of terrorism.

Pakistan was the seventh country to test nuclear weapons.

CHAPTER 8

ECONOMICS: SEEKING SELF-SUFFICIENCY

Pakistan is not a wealthy nation, and approximately 24 percent of its people live below the poverty level.[1] However, according to the Pakistani government, per capita income rose from $586 in 2002–2003 to $1,085 in 2007–2008.[2] That sharp increase was due mainly to payments sent home by Pakistanis working in foreign countries, such as Saudi Arabia, the United States, the United Kingdom, and the nations surrounding the Persian Gulf. The United States and other countries also increased aid to Pakistan during that time.

ECONOMIC ISSUES

Pakistan's economy has suffered from decades of internal political disputes, ongoing corruption, and a narrow focus on military and security.

Members of the Pakistan army unpack supplies for flood victims in August 2010. Pakistan is trying to become more self-sufficient.

In fact, that focus has harmed all aspects of Pakistani life. The country has also struggled to become economically self-sufficient, relying on foreign aid to assist in building its infrastructure, equipping its military, and feeding its people. Pakistan's most important export item—textiles—is threatened by competition from other countries, and no other product is being developed to replace it.

Runaway inflation has compounded Pakistan's economic problems, and the value of the Pakistani rupee (PKR) has been rapidly falling. In 2005, 59.52 PKR equaled one US dollar. Over the next several years, as the value of the PKR fell, the equivalent of US dollars rose. One dollar equaled 60.35 PKR in 2006, 70.64 PKR in 2008, and 85.27 PKR in 2010.[3]

PAKISTAN'S CURRENCY

The currency of Pakistan is the Pakistani rupee (PKR). The country's banknotes, which come in denominations between 5 and 5,000 rupees, were redesigned in the first decade of the twenty-first century, and the new bills have high-tech security features, including microletters and security threads. In addition, the new bills are machine readable, which means a bank can scan a note into a computer to ensure it is not counterfeit. Each denomination is a different color, but all the bills feature a portrait of Pakistan's founder, Mohammed Ali Jinnah.

TRADE

Besides textiles, Pakistan's other major exports include rice, sporting goods, chemicals, leather and leather goods, and carpets and rugs. All these items are highly dependent on water, a resource that is limited in Pakistan's arid landscape. In addition, the industries

Pakistani rupees

IRRIGATION

Pakistan has one of the largest irrigation systems in the world and little room to expand it further. Ironically, one of the problems facing this arid country is soil degradation due to overwatering. Today, most of Pakistan's irrigated land has reduced fertility caused by excess salt or waterlogging. Both of these conditions occur frequently in arid and semiarid lands because of the overwatering of crops and seepage from irrigation systems. Over time, the land becomes unable to support plants, which leads to desertification, a serious problem for Pakistan.

that make these items are all major polluters, using fertilizers and pesticides to grow the raw products and other chemicals to make the finished goods.

Pakistan's top export partners are the United States, the United Arab Emirates, Afghanistan, and the United Kingdom. Pakistan's top import partners are China, Saudi Arabia, the United Arab Emirates, and the United States. Pakistan's biggest imports include machinery, plastics, transportation equipment, edible oils, tea, petroleum and petroleum products, paper and paperboard, and iron and steel.

NATURAL RESOURCES

Pakistan has many economically important natural resources, but few of them are available in large quantities. Arable land is vital to the country's economy. Farms cover 28 percent of Pakistan, and they are watered by the largest irrigation system in the world.[4]

Children walk on a broken water pipeline in Karachi. Aging infrastructure wastes Pakistan's precious resources.

HEALTH ISSUES

Pakistan faces many challenges related to health and disease, including high rates of acute respiratory infection and malnutrition. In addition, Pakistan is one of only four places in the world where polio is still common. The disease is spreading, with 126 new cases reported in 2010.[5] The threat of polio has been worsened by the conflict in the nation's northwest and by overcrowding and poor sanitation from the widespread flooding of 2010.

Major food- and water-borne infectious diseases with a high degree of risk include bacterial diarrhea, hepatitis A and E, and typhoid fever. Dengue fever, malaria, and rabies are also present, as is the H5N1 avian influenza. Tuberculosis—the disease that killed Pakistan's beloved founder, Mohammed Ali Jinnah, in 1948—continues at a rate of 181 cases per 100,000 of population.[6] According to 2008 figures from the World Health Organization, Pakistan's government spends only US$7.00 per capita on health care.[7]

Salt and limestone are important natural resources as well. In addition to limestone, Pakistan produces some sandstone, granite, and marble, and there are minor deposits of iron ore and copper. The nation also exports some semiprecious and precious stones, most of which are found in Khyber Pakhtunkhwa and Gilgit Baltistan. Pakistan has few forests, so timber is very limited. The nation's demand for timber far outpaces what it produces.

Pakistan's natural gas reserves are quite large, although the gas that is produced is used only within the country and is not exported. Indeed, the country must import natural gas and oil to meet its energy demands. Coal is found in the country, but it is believed to be of poor quality.

In Pakistan's fishing industry, shrimp is the most important catch. The country also exports frozen fish, but the deep-sea fishing industry has stayed small because of a lack of appropriate fishing vessels. There is also a small-scale fishery in coastal waters that catches mako sharks, tuna, mackerel, marlin, sailfish, snapper, and grouper.

AGRICULTURE

Pakistan is a rapidly urbanizing farming nation, but 43 percent of its workers are still employed in agriculture.[8] Livestock makes up the largest part of the agricultural sector. Pakistan's leather industry is based on the production of buffalo, cow, goat, and sheep, and 75 percent of the raw materials, or hides, are supplied by the nation's livestock producers.[9]

Leather is one of the country's major export items, but the demand for leather products has fallen lately with the global recession in the first decade of the twenty-first century. Tanneries are also one of the major contributors to pollution in Pakistan and are directly connected to widespread environmental and health problems.

Important grain crops include wheat, rice, maize, millet, and barley. Pakistan's major and staple food crop is wheat. In past years, Pakistan had to import wheat to meet its daily food needs, but in 2010, the nation produced enough wheat to export the surplus. Rice is another major staple food crop, and several types are grown in Pakistan. Basmati rice, in particular, has become an important agricultural export. Chickpeas, cotton, and sugarcane are other major crops.

Farm fields in Khyber Pakhtunkhwa

Pakistan has numerous orchards and is known for its figs, mangoes, pomegranates, apricots, almonds, and pine nuts. Fresh and dried fruits are among its agricultural exports. Pakistanis also grow apples, peaches, pears, plums, and grapes.

TOURISM

Pakistan has many national parks and wildlife areas that offer examples of the country's varied landscape and environment. The northern mountains are a prime destination for trekkers and mountaineers who come to visit "the roof of the world." To the west are the trout streams of Khyber Pakhtunkhwa's cool and mostly green valleys. To the south, along Pakistan's coastal beaches, tourists enjoy swimming, beachcombing, picnicking, and horseback riding. From the high plains of Deosai National Park to the sand dunes and mud volcanoes of Hingol National Park, Jeep touring through the deserts and mountains is popular.

With landscapes to rival any on Earth, as well as an abundance of cultural and historical sites,

GROWING SEASONS

Pakistan has two agricultural growing seasons: the *karif*, or "autumn," season and the *rabi*, or "spring," season. Karif crops include rice, cotton, sugarcane, maize, pulses, and millets. They are planted in spring, before the monsoon rains, and harvested from October through December. Rabi crops include wheat, gram, lentil, tobacco, rapeseed, barley, and mustard. They are planted in autumn and harvested from April through May.

INFRASTRUCTURE

Number of airports: 148
World rank: 37

Railroads: 4,841 miles (7,791 km)
World rank: 28

Paved roads: 107,390 miles (172,827 km)

Unpaved roads: 53,668 miles (86,370 km)

Total roads: 161,058 miles (259,197 km)
World rank: 20[12]

Pakistan should be filled with tourists. Yet that is not the case. Incidents of civil unrest, including terrorist attacks and killings or kidnappings, have closed resorts, destroyed historic artifacts, and made travel unsafe in increasingly large areas of the country. Tourism has been declining since it reached a peak of 80,000 to 180,000 visitors annually in the 1980s and 1990s. Since the mid-1990s, annual tourism has dropped to 70,000 visitors or fewer. Only 6 percent of visitors to South Asia choose to visit Pakistan.[10]

Tourism was also hurt by the 2005 earthquake that hit Kashmir, and the decline was accelerated by the 2010 floods that destroyed many roads, bridges, and hotels. But the major loss of tourism in Pakistan has been due to terrorism. Estimates have placed the financial toll at 550 billion PKR, or approximately US$6.5 billion.[11]

Pakistan is trying to promote tourism. For example, in October 2010, the Department of Tourism announced it was dropping mountain

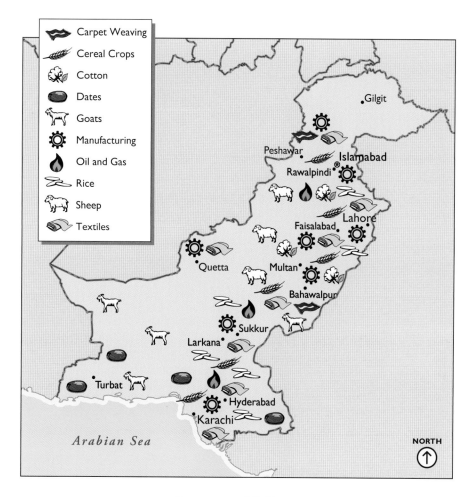

Resources of Pakistan

Legend:
- Carpet Weaving
- Cereal Crops
- Cotton
- Dates
- Goats
- Manufacturing
- Oil and Gas
- Rice
- Sheep
- Textiles

climbing fees for the 2011 season by 40 percent.[13] Even so, until Pakistan becomes more stable, it will have limited success in drawing visitors.

CHAPTER 9
PAKISTAN TODAY

Traffic, pollution, fast food, and shopping. For Pakistanis living in the city, life is similar to that of people in any modern urban area, with one exception: Pakistanis frequently face attacks by terrorists. Still, life goes on, and middle- and upper-class Pakistanis go to work and school.

LIFE AND EDUCATION

Lifestyles and gender roles in Pakistan vary with locale, economics, and education. For example, living in a well-to-do urban area of one of Pakistan's big cities in Punjab or Sindh Province is similar to living in the United States. Teens wear jeans and T-shirts, attend school, play computer games, text their friends, and listen to rock and rap music. Both males and females may go on to higher education, often attending universities overseas.

In Pakistan, the family elders are respected and given the choicest food and drink.

A young man sells Pakistani flags in Karachi. Pakistanis are proud of their country.

This lifestyle contrasts sharply with that in parts of western Pakistan's tribal area, where purdah is the norm. Under purdah, a woman must remain tightly veiled, and she cannot leave her house unless accompanied by a close male relative such as her father or husband. If she dishonors the family, her male relatives may kill her, a practice that occurs throughout the country.

Life may also be very different for poor and rural Pakistanis. Children are unlikely to attend school beyond a rudimentary stage. Fewer than half of Pakistani children continue their education through high school. Many children barely learn to read. Even though Pakistan's literacy rate has been climbing, the distribution is uneven across regions and among males and females.

Instead of attending school, many children go to work at ages as young as seven to ten. According to statistics from the US Department of Labor, 16.4 percent of children ten to 14 years of age work in Pakistan.[1] With certain

SCHOOLING

Attending high school is unlikely for most Pakistani students. According to World Bank figures, only 30 percent of students go on to secondary education, or schooling between the ages of ten and 16. That number drops to 19 percent for upper-secondary education.[2]

Teachers educate children of the urban poor in an outdoor street school in Karachi.

Pakistani women lead a march raising awareness for women's education.

exceptions, Pakistan has not established a minimum age for working.

Although illegal, bonded labor still exists in Pakistan. Bonded labor is a form of forced labor in which a family sells their child. Another form of forced labor involves the abduction and training of children as young as 11 to serve as suicide bombers for terrorist groups.

Young women in Pakistan's poor and rural regions are more likely to marry young. In Balochistan, for example, 62 percent of women marry before the age of 20. That percentage drops to 42 percent in Punjab.[3] A higher rate of adolescent marriage for young women is linked to a lack of education.

LITERACY RATES

The overall literacy rate in Pakistan, as estimated in 2005, is 49.9 percent, with 63 percent of men and 36 percent of women able to read and write.[4] However, an understanding of the disparity in literacy across the country comes from comparing information from FATA and Khyber Pakhtunkhwa, which border each other:

Literacy Rates, 2003

	Males	Females	Total
Khyber Pakhtunkhwa	51.39%	18.82%	35.41%
FATA	29.51%	3.00%	17.42%[5]

A CHANGING ENVIRONMENT

Pakistan is facing a myriad of environmental problems that intertwine with its economic difficulties. For instance, the nation's wetlands are an important natural resource for its people, livestock, and wildlife, supplying food, grazing, wood for fuel, and water for irrigation. Yet most of Pakistan's wetlands are not protected and are being threatened by development, pollution, exploitation, and a general lack of conservation practices. Many of the same concerns surround the nation's forest resources, which are threatened by deforestation due to population growth and development.

Desertification is a global problem and one that is of particular concern for Pakistan. Any loss of biodiversity, land productivity, or soil fertility will increase the country's poverty. Overgrazing and

2011

The first months of 2011 were plagued with increasing violence and terrorism. Pakistan began the year with the assassination of Punjab's liberal governor, Salman Taseer, who was pushing to amend the county's blasphemy laws. Then on January 12, a car bomb at a police station in northwest Pakistan killed 17 people.[6] On the same day, two Muslims were convicted under the blasphemy laws in Punjab Province and sentenced to life in prison. This may have been the first time, however, that a prison sentence was imposed, rather than a death sentence.[7]

Since Osama bin Laden was killed on May 2, terror attacks in Pakistan have increased.

desertification have ruined much of Pakistan's open rangeland, limiting livestock production. This has posed a serious problem for communities that depend on herd animals. As a result, many people have left their homes and migrated to urban areas.

PROBLEMS OF DEFINITION

One of Pakistan's ongoing problems is in defining itself and its form of government. Since shortly after gaining independence as an Islamic state, Pakistan has struggled to define itself as either a secular democracy or as an Islamic state, although the trend has been toward the latter. According to some estimates, at the time of the nation's partition in 1947, the number of madrassas in Pakistan was approximately 250. Today, some estimates place the number of madrassas as high as 45,000, with 15 percent of them preaching intolerance and hatred.[8] During 2010, an average of 100 people were killed each month in suicide bombings in Pakistan.[9] This level of violence is a dangerous condition in an unstable country that also possesses nuclear weapons.

Pakistan has had a recurring problem with corruption. Many of its leaders, including Benazir Bhutto, have been charged with corruption or other illegal acts. Many members of the government and the army use their positions to increase their personal wealth and power. Although there are government agencies working to address the problem, little progress has been made. Pakistan's founder, Mohammed Ali Jinnah, recognized this problem from the nation's very beginning. As he stated in his address to the Constituent Assembly, "One of the biggest curses from which [we are] suffering—I do not say that other countries are free from it, but, I think, our condition is much worse—is bribery and corruption."[10]

Since independence, Pakistan has struggled to achieve stability. Its economy remains underdeveloped, and many of its people live in poverty. Tribal and religious factions clash, and the tension often leads to violence. The nation's scarce natural resources are becoming ever scarcer, due to overuse and environmental challenges. And its rapidly growing population makes facing all of these challenges more difficult.

Nonetheless, through decades of turmoil and military rule, the Pakistani people have repeatedly reaffirmed their commitment to their democratic system of government. Their resilience and basic desire to work together shows promise for their nation's future.

Faisal Mosque in Islamabad serves as Pakistan's national mosque. Pakistan still struggles to define itself as an Islamic democracy.

TIMELINE

500,000 years ago	Stone Age people form stone tools such as hand axes in the Rohri Hills.
2500 BCE	The Indus River valley culture occupies most of Pakistan, from the foothills of the Himalayas to the Arabian Sea.
326 BCE	Alexander the Great crosses the Indus River and assumes control of Pakistan.
600 BCE	The city of Taxila, a center for Buddhist learning, is founded.
700s CE	Mohammad bin Qasim leads the first Islamic invasion of Pakistan.
1707	Mughal emperor Aurangzeb dies on March 3, effectively ending Mughal domination.
1799	Ranjit Singh seizes Lahore and soon unites all of Punjab.
1850s	The British consolidate their control over the Indian subcontinent.
1906	The All India Muslim League is founded.
1947	On August 14, the United Kingdom gives India independence and partitions it into predominantly Hindu India and predominantly Islamic Pakistan.
1948	Mohammed Ali Jinnah, Pakistan's first governor-general, dies on September 11.
1956	Pakistan's first constitution is instituted on February 29, and Iskander Mirza becomes Pakistan's first president.

1958	On October 7, Mirza declares martial law and nullifies the constitution.
1971	On December 16, Pakistani forces surrender to Indian forces, ending the conflict in East Pakistan and creating Bangladesh.
1973	On August 14, Pakistan's new constitution is enacted, and Zulfikar Ali Bhutto becomes prime minister.
1977	On July 5, Muhammad Zia-ul-Haq instigates a coup, removing Bhutto's government and declaring martial law.
1988	On December 2, Benazir Bhutto becomes prime minister.
1999	On October 12, Pervez Musharraf leads a coup and seizes control of Pakistan.
2005	On October 8, an earthquake kills tens of thousands of people.
2007	On December 27, former prime minister Benazir Bhutto is assassinated in Rawalpindi.
2008	On August 18, Musharraf resigns as Pakistan's president. On September 9, Benazir Bhutto's widower, Asif Ali Zardari, is sworn in as president.
2010	In July and August, Pakistan is hit by the worst flooding in decades, affecting 20 million people.
2011	On January 4, Salman Taseer, the governor of Punjab Province, is assassinated.
2011	On May 2, US forces locate and kill al-Qaeda leader Osama bin Laden in Abbottabad.

FACTS AT YOUR FINGERTIPS

GEOGRAPHY

Official name: Islamic Republic of Pakistan (in Urdu, Islami Jumhuria Pakistan)

Area: 307,374 square miles (796,095 sq km)

Climate: Arid, mostly hot dry desert, temperate in the northwest, arctic in the northern mountains.

Highest elevation: Chogori, or K2, 28,251 feet (8,611 m) above sea level

Lowest elevation: Arabian Sea, 0 feet (0 m) below sea level

Significant geographic features: K2, several of the world's other highest mountains, Indus River

PEOPLE

Population (July 2011 est.): 187,342,721

Most populous city: Karachi

Ethnic groups: Punjabi, 44.68 percent; Pashtun, 15.42 percent; Sindhi, 14.1 percent; Seraiki, 8.38 percent; Muhajirs, 7.57 percent; Balochi, 3.57 percent; other, 6.28 percent

Percentage of residents living in urban areas: 36 percent

Life expectancy: 65.99 years at birth (world rank: 166)

Language(s): Punjabi, 48 percent; Sindhi, 12 percent; Seraiki (a Punjabi variant), 10 percent; Urdu (official), 8 percent; Pashto, 8 percent; Balochi, 3 percent; Hindko, 2 percent; Brahui, 1 percent; English (official; lingua franca of Pakistani elite and most government ministries), Burushaski, and other, 8 percent

Religion(s): Islam, 95 percent (including Sunni, 75 percent, and Shia, 20 percent); other (including Christianity and Hinduism), 5 percent

GOVERNMENT AND ECONOMY

Government: federal republic

Capital: Islamabad

Date of adoption of current constitution: April 12, 1973 (has since been suspended, restored, and amended multiple times)

Head of state: president

Head of government: prime minister

Legislature: Majlis-e-Shoora, consists of the National Assembly and the Senate

Currency: Pakistani rupee (PKR)

Industries and natural resources: Textiles (including garments, bed

linens, cotton cloth, yarn), rice, leather goods, sporting goods, chemicals, carpets and rugs

NATIONAL SYMBOLS

Holidays: As an Islamic nation, Pakistan observes Islamic holy days. In addition, its national holidays include Pakistan Day on March 23, which commemorates the Lahore Resolution; Independence Day on August 14; Muhammad Iqbal's birthday on November 9; and Mohammed Ali Jinnah's birthday on December 25.

Flag: Green background with a white band down the left side and a white crescent and star, representing Islam, in the center

National anthem: "Qaumi Tarana" ("National Anthem"), adopted in 1954

National animal: markhor goat

National bird: chukar

KEY PEOPLE

Mohammed Ali Jinnah (1876–1948), considered the father of Pakistan

Muhammad Iqbal (1877–1938), considered the national poet

Benazir Bhutto (1953–2007), the first female prime minister

PROVINCES AND REGIONS OF PAKISTAN

Province; Capital

Balochistan; Quetta

Khyber Pakhtunkhwa; Peshawar

Punjab; Lahore

Sindh; Karachi

Federally Administered Region; Capital

Azad Kashmir; Muzaffarabad

Federally Administered Tribal Area (FATA); no capital, region is governed by multiple agencies

Gilgit Baltistan; Gilgit

Islamabad Capital Territory; Islamabad

GLOSSARY

annex

To incorporate an area or territory into an existing one.

arable

Fertile and fit for agriculture.

autocracy

A system of government in which one person holds all the power.

blasphemous

Disrespectful of religion.

burka

A loose garment with veiled holes to see through; worn by some Islamic women in public.

desertification

The process by which fertile land becomes desert.

guerrilla

A rebel or revolutionary.

ibex

A type of wild goat with long, curved horns that generally inhabits rocky, mountainous terrain.

inflation

An increase in prices and a fall in the purchasing value of money.

jihad

A religious struggle; commonly used to refer to an Islamic holy war.

martial law

Temporary rule by military authorities during a declared state of emergency; government activities and individual rights are usually suspended.

oligarchy

A system of government in which a small group holds all the power.

paramilitary

A nongovernment force similar to a military.

patriarchal

Ruled by men or fathers.

purdah

The Islamic custom of keeping women in seclusion.

scimitar

A sword with a curved blade.

secular

Nonreligious.

stupa

A Buddhist monument based on the form of ancient burial mounds.

tanneries

Facilities for turning animal hide into leather.

waterlogging

A rise in the water table that causes oversaturation of the soil.

ADDITIONAL RESOURCES

SELECTED BIBLIOGRAPHY

Cohen, Stephen Philip. *The Idea of Pakistan.* Washington, DC: Brookings Institute, 2004. Print.

Khan, Yasmin. *The Great Partition: The Making of India and Pakistan.* New Haven, CT: Yale UP, 2007. Print.

Rashid, Ahmed. *Descent into Chaos: The United States and the Failure of Nation Building in Pakistan, Afghanistan, and Central Asia.* New York: Viking Penguin, 2008. Print.

Talbott, Strobe. *Engaging India: Diplomacy, Democracy, and the Bomb.* Washington, DC: Brookings Institute, 2004. Print.

FURTHER READINGS

Mortenson, Greg. *Three Cups of Tea: One Man's Mission to Promote Peace . . . One School at a Time.* New York: Penguin, 2007. Print.

Staples, Suzanne Fisher. *Shabanu: Daughter of the Wind.* New York: Laurel Leaf, 2003. Print.

WEB LINKS

To learn more about Pakistan, visit ABDO Publishing Company online at
www.abdopublishing.com. Web sites about Pakistan are featured on our
Book Links page. These links are routinely monitored and updated to provide the
most current information available.

PLACES TO VISIT

If you are ever in Pakistan, consider checking out these important and interesting sites!

Faisal Mosque

The national mosque of Pakistan is located in Islamabad.

Khunjerab National Park

Located on the border with China in Gilgit Baltistan, this national park is a great
place to see Pakistan's fascinating wildlife.

Mohenjo Daro

Located in Sindh, this ancient city was the center of the Indus River valley
civilization.

SOURCE NOTES

CHAPTER 1. A VISIT TO PAKISTAN

1. Michael Palin. *Himalaya*. New York: Thomas Dunne, 2005. 44. *Google Book Search*. Web. 26 Apr. 2011.

CHAPTER 2. GEOGRAPHY: A RUGGED LAND

1. "The World Factbook: Pakistan." *Central Intelligence Agency*. Central Intelligence Agency, 6 Apr. 2011. Web. 26 Apr. 2011.

2. "K2." *Encyclopædia Britannica*. Encyclopædia Britannica, 2011. Web. 26 Apr. 2011.

3. "Historic World Earthquakes: Pakistan." *US Geological Survey: Earthquake Hazards Program*. USGS, 2011. Web. 26 Apr. 2011.

4. "Mountain Tourism in Iran." *Embassy of Pakistan in Iran*. Embassy of Pakistan in Iran, n.d. Web. 26 Apr. 2011.

5. "Basic Facts." *Ministry of Information and Broadcasting*. Government of Pakistan, n.d. Web. 26 Apr. 2011.

6. "Country Guide: Pakistan." *BBC: Weather*. BBC, n.d. Web. 25 Apr. 2011.

7. "Mean Annual Rainfall." *Pakistan Meteorological Department*. Government of Pakistan, n.d. Web. 26 Apr. 2011.

8. "State of the Climate: Global Hazards, August 2010." *National Climatic Data Center and National Oceanic and Atmospheric Administration, National Environmental Satellite, Data, and Information Service*. US Department of Commerce, Aug. 2010. Web. 26 Apr. 2011.

CHAPTER 3. ANIMALS AND NATURE: DIVERSE AND ELUSIVE

1. "Mammals of Pakistan." *Wildlife of Pakistan*. Wildlife of Pakistan, 2004. Web. 26 Apr. 2011.

2. "Reptiles of Pakistan." *Wildlife of Pakistan*. Wildlife of Pakistan, 2004. Web. 26 Apr. 2011.

3. "Section Seven: Forests of Pakistan." *Wildlife of Pakistan*. Wildlife of Pakistan, 2004. Web. 26 Apr. 2011.

4. "Summary Statistics: Summaries by Country, Table 5, Threatened Species in Each Country." *IUCN Red List of Threatened Species*. International Union for Conservation of Nature and Natural Resources, 2010. Web. 27 Apr. 2011.

5. "Deosai National Park." *Wildlife of Pakistan*. Wildlife of Pakistan, 2004. Web. 26 Apr. 2011.

6. "Moschus chrysogaster." *IUCN Red List of Threatened Species*. International Union for Conservation of Nature and Natural Resources, 2010. Web. 26 Apr. 2011.

7. "Toxins from Tanneries Endangering Kasur's Residents." *Daily Times* (Pakistan). Daily Times, 3 May 2007. Web. 27 Apr. 2011.

8. "Khunjerab National Park." *World Wildlife Fund*. World Wildlife Fund, n.d. Web. 26 Apr. 2011.

CHAPTER 4. HISTORY: STRIVING FOR STABILITY

1. "The World Factbook: Pakistan." *Central Intelligence Agency*. Central Intelligence Agency, 6 Apr. 2011. Web. 26 Apr. 2011.

CHAPTER 5. PEOPLE: TRIBAL TRADITIONS

1. Stephen Philip Cohen. *The Idea of Pakistan*. Washington, DC: Brookings Institute, 2004. Print. 271.

2. "The World Factbook: Pakistan." *Central Intelligence Agency*. Central Intelligence Agency, 6 Apr. 2011. Web. 26 Apr. 2011.

3. "Pakistan Economic Survey 2009–10: Population, Labour Force, and Employment." *Ministry of Finance*. Government of Pakistan, 2010. Web. 27 Apr. 2011.

4. "The World Factbook: Pakistan." *Central Intelligence Agency*. Central Intelligence Agency, 6 Apr. 2011. Web. 26 Apr. 2011.

5. Ibid.

6. Ibid.

7. "Pakistan: Massacre of Minority Ahmadis." *Human Rights Watch*. Human Rights Watch, 1 June 2010. Web. 26 May 2011.

CHAPTER 6. CULTURE: A COLORFUL NATION

1. "Pakistan." *Database Olympics*. Database Olympics, 2011. Web. 27 Apr. 2011.

CHAPTER 7. POLITICS: DEMOCRATIC IDEALS

1. "Mr. Jinnah's Presidential Address to the Constituent Assembly of Pakistan, August 11, 1947." *Pakistani.org*. Pakistani.org, n.d. Web. 27 Apr. 2011.

2. "Objectives Resolution." *Story of Pakistan*. Enterprise Team, 1 June 2003. Web. 27 Apr. 2011.

3. "Background Note: Pakistan." *US Department of State*. US Department of State, 6 Oct. 2010. Web. 27 May 2011.

CHAPTER 8. ECONOMICS: SEEKING SELF-SUFFICIENCY

1. "The World Factbook: Pakistan." *Central Intelligence Agency*. Central Intelligence Agency, 6 Apr. 2011. Web. 26 Apr. 2011.

2. "Salient Features of Pakistan's Economy." *Ministry of Finance*. Government of Pakistan, 11 June 2008. Web. 27 May 2011.

3. "The World Factbook: Pakistan." *Central Intelligence Agency*. Central Intelligence Agency, 6 Apr. 2011. Web. 26 Apr. 2011.

4. "Background Note: Pakistan." *US Department of State*. US Department of State, 6 Oct. 2010. Web. 27 Apr. 2011.

5. "UNICEF: Crisis Far from Over for Pakistan's Children." *UNICEF*. UNICEF, 7 Dec. 2010. Web. 27 Apr. 2011.

6. "Infectious Diseases: Pakistan." *USAID*. USAID, 22 Sept. 2009. Web. 27 Apr. 2011.

7. "Demographic Indicators: Pakistan." *World Health Organization Country Profiles*. World Health Organization, Aug. 2010. Web. 27 Apr. 2011.

8. "The World Factbook: Pakistan." *Central Intelligence Agency*. Central Intelligence Agency, 6 Apr. 2011. Web. 26 Apr. 2011.

9. Amanullah Bashar. "Leather Industry: Difficult Times." *Pakistan and Gulf Economist*. Pakistan and Gulf Economist, 27 Apr. 2003. Web. 27 Apr. 2011.

10. "Country Profile: Pakistan." *Library of Congress*. Library of Congress, Federal Research Division, Feb. 2005. Web. 26 Apr. 2011.

11. "Terrorism Cost Rs.550 bn to Tourism Sector." *Associated Press of Pakistan*. APP, 17 Jan. 2011. Web. 27 Apr. 2011.

12. "The World Factbook: Pakistan." *Central Intelligence Agency*. Central Intelligence Agency, 6 Apr. 2011. Web. 26 Apr. 2011.

13. "Ministry of Tourism, Government of Pakistan Has Decided to Give 40 Percent Discount on Royalty Fee on All Peaks." *Ministry of Tourism*. Government of Pakistan, 5 Oct. 2010. Web. 27 May 2011.

CHAPTER 9. PAKISTAN TODAY

1. "Pakistan." *US Department of Labor's 2009 Findings on the Worst Forms of Child Labor*. US Department of Labor, Bureau of International Labor Affairs, 15 Dec. 2010. Web. 27 Apr. 2011.

2. "Education in Pakistan." *World Bank*. World Bank Group, 2011. Web. 27 May 2011.

3. Munawar Santana. "Culture of Silence: A Brief on Reproductive Health of Adolescents and Youth in Pakistan." *Population Council*. Population Council, 2005. Web. 27 Apr. 2011.

4. "The World Factbook: Pakistan." *Central Intelligence Agency*. Central Intelligence Agency, 6 Apr. 2011. Web. 26 Apr. 2011.

5. "Socio Economic Indicators." *Federally Administered Tribal Areas, FATA Secretariat*. FATA, n.d. Web. 27 Apr. 2011.

6. "Pakistani Bomber Kills 17 in Attack on Police." *BBC News*. BBC, 12 Jan. 2011. Web. 27 May 2011.

7. "Life in Jail for Two Pakistani Muslim Blasphemers." *BBC News*. BBC, 12 Jan. 2011. Web. 27 May 2011.

8. Peter W. Singer. "Pakistan's Madrassahs: Ensuring a System of Education Not Jihad." *Brookings*. Brookings Institution, 1 Nov. 2001. Web. 27 Apr. 2011.

9. Sanjeev Miglani. "Suicide Bombings in Afghanistan: The Bloodiest Year." *Afghan Journal*. Reuters, 26 Dec. 2010. Web. 27 Apr. 2011.

10. "Mr. Jinnah's Presidential Address to the Constituent Assembly of Pakistan, August 11, 1947." *Pakistani.org*. Pakistani.org, n.d. Web. 27 Apr. 2011.

INDEX

INDEX CONTINUED

PHOTO CREDITS